Urban/Nanopoulos
Information and Management

Sabine Urban/Constantin Nanopoulos (eds.)

Information and Management

Utilization of Technology – Structural and Cultural Impact

With the contributions of:

Hanns A. Abele, Paolo Bertoletti, Yves De Ronge,
Adamantios Diamantopoulos & Anne Laure Souchon,
Constantinos Markides & Elizabeth A.M. Tracy,
Constantin Nanopoulos, Giovanni Palmerio,
Markku Saaksjarvi

GABLER

Sabine Urban is a Professor at Strasburg University (Robert Schuman) and heads the CESAG (Centre of Managerial Research)/I.E.C.S. which is affiliated to it. She teaches international economics and corporate strategies in several universities both in France and abroad, and is in charge of the International Commerce degree at the I.E.C.S.- European Management School. She sits on the board of several industrial and financial firms. Her main research fields are International Business and European economy.

Constantin Nanopoulos is a Senior Lecturer in Statistics at Strasburg University (Robert Schuman). He received a Doctor's Degree in Mathematics from the University of Strasburg (Louis Pasteur) in 1977 and moved to Habilitation in Management Sciences in 1994. His main fields of research are International Business, Statistics, InformationSystems and Information and Communication Technologies.

Acknowledgement
The editor is grateful to the Société des Amis des Université de l'Académie de Strasbourg and to the Conseil Général du Bas-Rhin for their financial support.

Die Deutsche Bibliothek - CIP-Einheitsaufnahme
Information and management : utilization of technology – structural and cultural impact / Sabine Urban/Constantin Nanopoulos (eds.). With the contributions of: Hanns A. Abele ...
- Wiesbaden : Gabler, 1998

Gabler Verlag is a subsidiary company of Bertelsmann Professional Information

ISBN-13:978-3-409-12264-1   e-ISBN-13:978-3-322-86995-1
DOI: 10.1007/978-3-322-86995-1

Preface

The current work is the sixth volume in the Series "Europe's Economic Future", edited by Strasbourg's Robert Schuman University, under the direction of Professor Sabine URBAN, head of the CESAG-IECS research center.

The authors have in common the fact that they have each participated in the work of the CESAG as visiting professors at Robert Schuman University during the 1996-97 academic year and, in most cases, took part in the 3rd Colloquium organized by the AIM ("Association Information et Management" or Information and Management Association) held in Strasbourg May 28-30, 1997 under the direction of Kostas Nanopoulos with the support of Eurostat and the European Community.

The subject matter of the current work is highly topical because it deals with fundamental changes in the organization of work and in daily work routines. The new information and communication technologies discussed raise fundamental issues in the management of organizations, and also in ethical questions, and do so on a worldwide scale.

The Editors

Contents

Contributors

<table>
<tr><td>Hanns A. Abele</td><td>received a Doctor's Degree in Law from the University of Vienna in 1963 and moved on to Habilitation (economics) there in 1972. He was appointed full professor (economics) at the University of Fribourg, Switzerland in 1973. Currently he is full professor (political economy) at the University of Economics and Business Administration Vienna. He taught at various academic institutions and was a Fulbright Scholar in 1987/88. Being a member of a number of scientific organizations he was elected president of the Fribourg Working Group for Broadcasting Economics in 1992. Among his fields of interest are money and credit, finance, theory of economic policy, cultural economics, and media economics. In these areas he published books and articles in journals. Besides his interests in theoretical economics he has been active in computer based instruction for more than a decade.</td></tr>
<tr><td>Paolo Bertoletti</td><td>born in 1963, is Ricercatore at the Dipartimento di economia politica e metodi quantitativi, University of Pavia. He received his MPhil. in Economics from the University of Oxford, and his Dottorato in economia politica from the University of Pavia. His main fields of research are Industrial Organization and The Economic Theory of Regulation. He teaches Microeconomics in Pavia and at the Libero Istituto Universitario Cattaneo of Castellanza.</td></tr>
<tr><td>Yves De Rongé</td><td>is Professor of Management Control at the Université Catholique de Louvain (UCL), Belgium since 1991 and is Invited Professor at Facultés Universitaires Saint Louis (Brussels) and at the Katholieke Universiteit Leuven. He holds a MBA from the University of Chicago and a PhD in applied economics from</td></tr>
</table>

UCL. His research interests are in the field of innovations in management accounting systems and in the field of the cultural and international aspects of management control.

Adamantios Diamantopoulos is Professor of Marketing and Business Research and Director of Research at Loughborough University Business School (UK). His research interests are in pricing, sales forecasting, marketing research, and international marketing and he is the author of some 150 publications in these areas. He has presented his research at more than 50 international conferences and has been the recipient of several Best Paper Awards. His work has appeared, among others, in *the International Journal of Research in Marketing, International Journal of Forecasting* and *International Business Review*. He sits on the editorial review boards of seven marketing journals, is a founder member of the Consortium for International Marketing Research (CIMaR), Associate Editor of the *International Journal of Research in Marketing*, and a referee for several academic journals, professional associations and funding bodies.

Anne L. Souchon is a Lecturer in Marketing at the School of Business and Public Management at Victoria University of Wellington (New Zealand). Her research interests have been mainly in the areas of international/export marketing and information utilisation. Her work has been published in several academic outlets including the *Journal of International Marketing*, the *Journal of Marketing Management, Advances in International Marketing,* and various conference proceedings (such as those of the American Marketing Association and the Academy of International Business). Her research has also been presented at several international conferences worldwide.

Constantinos C. Markides is Associate Professor of Strategic and International Management and the past Director of the *Accelerated Development Programme* at the London Business School. A native of Cyprus, he received his BA (Distinction) and MA in Economics from Boston University, and his MBA and DBA from the Harvard Business School. He has worked as an Associate with the Cyprus Development Bank and as a Research Associate at the Harvard Business School. He has done research and published on the topics of international competitiveness, corporate restructuring, refocusing and international acquisitions. His publications have appeared in journals such as the *Harvard Business Review, Directors & Boards, Long Range Planning, British Journal of Management, Journal of International Business Studies, Strategic Management Journal* and the *Academy of Management Journal.* His book *Diversification, Refocusing and Economic Performance* was published by MIT Press in December 1995 and his book *Crafting Strategy: A Journey into the Mind of the Strategist* will be published by Harvard Business School Press in 1997.

Elizabeth A.M. Tracy received her PhD degree from London Business School in July 1997. She is currently a Visiting Teaching Fellow at the Stern School of Business of New-York University.

Constantin Nanopoulos is a Senior Lecturer in Statistics at Strasburg University (Robert Schuman). He received a Doctor's Degree in Mathematics from the University of Strasburg (Louis Pasteur) in 1977 and moved to Habilitation in Management Sciences in 1994. He is a founding member of AIM (Association Information et Management). His mains fields of research are International Business, Statistics, Informations Systems and Information and Communication Technologies. He is author of numerous publications in these fields.

Giovanni Palmerio

born in 1941, he studied at the Universities of Bologna and Cambridge. He taught at the Universities of Ancona, Venice and Naples. Since 1976 he has been Full Professor of Economics at the Libera Università Internazionale degli Studi Sociali (LUISS Guido Carli) of Rome, where he is also Head of the Department of Economics. Since 1990 he has been President of the Italian Institute for Economic Forecasts (ISCO). He wrote books and articles on the business cycle, growth and development, public finance and inflation.

Markku Saaksjarvi

is a Professor of Information Systems at the Helsinki School of Economics and Business Administration. His research interests include strategic management of information technology, success evaluation of information systems, development strategies for information products, and electronic commerce.

Sabine Urban

is a Professor at Strasburg University (Robert Schuman) and heads the CESAG (Centre of Managerial Research)/IECS Strasbourg which is affiliated to it. She teaches international economics and corporate strategies in several universities both in France and abroad, and is in charge of the International Commerce degree at the IECS Strasbourg. She sits on the board of several industrial and financial firms. Her main research fields are International Business and the European economy; she is author and co-author of numerous publications in these fields.

Sabine Urban
and Constantin Nanopoulos

Information and Management: A Radical Evolution

1. Introduction

2. Evolution of information management

3. Strategic and operational changes introduced by the use of new information and communication technologies within companies

   A. Strategic choices
   B. Organizational control
   C. Information and operational performance

4. Information systems and organizational structures

5. Conclusion

1. Introduction

Since the earliest times, systems of information management are at the heart of organizations from whence they determine the nature of influence, power and efficiency. This observation is valid for political and religious institutions, military systems, and economic organizations. What is new today is the extra-ordinary intrusion of technology. Although we call this technology "new", modern life has been transformed since the beginning of the century by "new" information and communication technologies, powerfully shaped by the world wars.

Technology appears, in fact, to be a key factor in the economic growth and wealth of nations; it supports a society's will to change; it enables the orientation of structural modifications of the social system and the construction of the future[1]; it is the expression of human creativity. The evolution of technology brings with it a fear of the future; the expression of this realization found a place in the media with the 1972 MIT report "Limits of Growth" by Donella and Dennis Meadows, Jörgens Randers and William Behrens[2].

Today, it is not the fear of growth which dominates but rather a sort of fascination with "new" technology nourished by the observation that radical changes are powered by the application of new information and communication technologies. We talk henceforth of the "information age". From the individual use of computers, we have moved to information systems and, from there, on to interconnected networks allowing us to "navigate" around the world thanks to a "World Wide Web"[3]. The demand for information technology

---

[1] "Construire l'avenir" is the expression of Gaston Berger, founder in France of the *Prospective* review.

[2] *The Limits of Growth,* MIT, Boston, 1972.

[3] A global analysis of this evolution can be found in the publications of the OCDE: *Perspectives des technologies de l'information*, Paris, 1997; *L'Oberservateur de l'OCDE*, N° 206, June-July 1997; as well as in the works of Robert Reix, *Systèmes d'information et management des organisations*, Vuibert, Paris, 1995 or of Arnold Picot, Ralf Reichwald, Robert Wigand, *Die grenzenlose Unternehmung: Information, Organisation und Management*, Gabler, Wiesbaden, 1996.

is developing at an exponential rate and creates from day to day new activities and new needs. Existing organizational structures are rapidly being questioned at every level, micro-, macro- and meta-economic. The educational systems for training, modes of managing, and ethical considerations have all been profoundly transformed. The process of adapting to and anticipating change will be enhaced from now on.

The current work aims to illustrate this phenomenon by focusing observations and reflections along three lines: information technology proper, its utilization in enterprises to reach strategic and operational goals, and its structural and cultural impact.

2. Evolution of information management

"Information is that which brings us knowledge, modifies our vision of the world, reduces our uncertainty; it is a useful piece of advice" (Reix, 1995, p. 16). This information results from signals and data. It is a group of symbols that can be perceived by human beings or by a more limited component of a human being such as an individual cell. Fundamentally, information can be likened to an energy flow whose function is to regulate. This function can be targeted to reach a predetermined objective: in fact, every decision-making process is a process of converting information into action, according to J.W. Forrester[4]. The effectiveness of an action is a function of quality information. Information alone is not, however, sufficient to arrive at a rational decision. Rational decision making requires, among other things, a capacity to assimilate information and judicious reasoning[5]. Nonetheless, reliable information is a necessary, if not sufficient, condition for the process of effective decision-making. It is for this reason that access to information, combined with a capacity for logical analysis, is a source of power for individuals and for organizations. As a consequence individuals and companies which pick up, classify and diffuse information have

---

4   Forrester, J.W. (1961): *Industrial Dynamics*, Wiley, New York.

5   See Zeckhauser, R.J./Keeney, R.L./Sebenius, J.K. (1996): *Wise Choices; Decisions, Games and Negotiations*, Harvard Business School Press, Boston.

a considerable responsibility to the larger society. Information has a price; but it is fragile and carries a margin for error and time-sensitivity and represents a potential intrusion of privacy. Its communication then poses a great number of problems before we even consider the fact that interconnected information networks such as the WWW have become technically difficult to control. These networks have, however, the technical capacity to invade the world of primary information, accelerate access time and introduce new data at a prodigious rate. The technological architecture of information systems, even as it is harmonized according to largely accepted international norms, risks not corresponding to the real needs of users who may become literally suffocated by an excess of information. This leads to the question of treating or processing information before it is diffused, but using what rules, following which methods? Management models of companies will be refined perhaps, but certainly not simplified. The recognition of the complexity of reality, its revelation through more numerous and more accurate information, will only lead to a reduction in the degree of uncertainty faced by decision-makers will have to consider. We know that the human brain has a capacity to absorb and to master information which is not infinite. We are confronted then with a new need for simplification. Will we, with sophisticated techniques, succeed in accessing the essential pieces of information from a broad base of data?

Constantin Nanopoulos discusses some of the major challenges which relate to this question in the following chapter entitled "Future Changes in Statistical Record Keeping".

3. Strategic and operational changes introduced by the use of new information and communication technologies within companies

A. Strategic choices

Strategic management is a relatively new discipline whose emergence is generally dated to the mid-1960's with the ground-breaking work of Ansoff (1965), Anthony (1965) and Learned, Christensen, Andrews and Guth (LCAG model, 1965). The discipline was institutionalized in 1980 with the creation of the Strategic Management Society, and its spread was encouraged, by in particular, the writings of Michael Porter. The concepts were enriched by the contributions of organizational theory, industrial economics, game theory, system theory, and psycho-sociology. But the realization of the complex and paradoxical nature of strategic management led to a criticism of current strategic activity. Mintzberg (1994) analyzed the "grandeur and the decadence of strategic planification"[6] and led to a rather cynical view of information systems which he considered too formal, too backward-looking, too quantitative, and unreliable[7]. More recently, Gaddis (1997) appears equally incisive in "Strategy Under Attack"[8]. Gérard Koenig (1990, p. 67)[9] emphasizes in terms of strategy the "merits of a makeshift approach" enabling one to intelligently utilize resources of information, memory and imagination.

These references are mentioned here in order to emphasize how much information collected can at the same time reinforce convictions and, on the contrary, sow seeds of doubt. But evolution does not stop there: important transformations are in progress. Two vice presidents of the Boston Consulting Group (BCG) illustrate fundamental changes now in progress relating to strategies for the "new economy of information"[10]: new information technologies are reversing the behaviour of the players, their relationships, their relative bargaining power, market structures, competitive advantages, the organization of companies, the deconstruction of value chains, and configurations of hierarchical power structures. Every aspect of strategic management is in a state of rupture compared to the past. Markku Saaksjarvi goes beyond this realization in Chapter 3 which follows, entitled "Product Platform and IT Infrastructure in Strategic Management of IT", by demonstrating not only that fundamental

---

6   Mintzberg, H. (1994): *The Rise and Fall of Strategic Planning*, The Free Press, New York.

7   see op. cit, French translation, Dunod, 1994, p. 270.

8   Gaddis, P.O. (1997): Strategy Under Attack, *Long Range Planning*, Vol. 30, N° 1, pp. 38-45.

9   Koenig, G. (1990): *Management stratégique; Vison, manoeuvres et tactiques*, Nathan, Paris.

10   Evans, P.B. & Wurster, T. (1997): Strategy and the New Economics of Information, *Harvard Business Review*, Sept.-Oct., pp. 71-82.

changes, propelled by new information technologies (IT), are taking place but also that they will play a structural role in the future, limiting the breadth of the strategic choice that companies have. To a certain extent, it is no longer strategy which structures the organization of information but the opposite: the strategy of a firm is constrained by the (expensive!) information systems which are put in place. Decisions made in the area of information and communication condition new models of firms' development. The following terms have real meaning: cultural and economic "revolution", "product platforms", technological "architecture" and infrastructure, "virtual organizations", and "networks of informational competence" - all these are emerging concepts which will shape competitive advantages and entry barriers in the future.

B.   Organizational control

The development of new information and communication technologies, as mentioned above, leads to modification of a company's strategies for adapting to and anticipating change. From this position, there must necessarily be revisions to control systems. Yves De Rongé, in Chapter 4 which follows ("The Impact of New Information Systems") gives answers to questions relating to the impact of information technology on organizational change. An important evolution is in progress.

The first introduction of information technology in organizations allowed the automation of the organization according to its functional lines while more recent information and communication technologies are better suited to sustaining a process view of the organization.

In terms of management control, the author refers to the traditional definition of R. Anthony which distinguishes three levels of control in an organization: strategic planning, management control and task control. Strategic planning is defined as the process of deciding on the goals of the organization and the strategies for attaining these goals. Management control is the process by which managers influence other members of the organization to implement the organization's strategies. Task control is the process of assuring that specified tasks are carried out effectively and efficiently.

The objective of controlling the implementation of overall strategies by the members of the organization assigned to management control has two main consequences on its structure. Substrategies must have:
– consistency with organizational structure;
– coherence with the strategy chosen by the organizational unit.

In a functional organization (Taylorian view) the firm is seen as a set of independent functions regrouping similar competencies that are optimized locally according to their specialized competencies. Communication between functions is unusual and occurs only between the various functional top managers. Coordination is achieved at the top of the organization. Interdependencies between functions are weak and are managed and coordinated by the hierarchy. This type of organization is based on a top down approach of command and control.

Since the seventies, major developments in the economy and in technology have lead to a growing questioning of the relevance and adequacy of the functional organization for actual business challenges. Major changes in the economic environment have led to the need for alternative forms of organizational structure that take into account the cross-functional dimension of business. Nowadays, a firm can be seen as a set of processes that regroup a set of activities. An activity is a set of related tasks conducted by an entity of the organization. A process can be defined as a set of activities linked to one another by significant information flows and combined with one another to provide an important and well defined tangible or intangible product. A major characteristic of the processes is that they are made cross functional by linking together different activities that are undertaken in organizational units that belong to different functions.

In a rapidly changing environment, and with the adoption of a process view of the organization, management control systems need to be redefined in order to help manage continuous change instead of the historic experience of relative stability in business conditions. Recent developments in information and communication technologies have greatly enhanced the possibility of developing management control systems which are well adapted to the informational needs of the process organization. Several developments in information and communication technologies have made this possible, especially:

- integrated software;
- groupware technologies;
- Internet and intranets;
- data warehousing.

De Rongé shows that there is a high coherence between the new possibilities opened by the development of New Information and Communication Technologies (NICT) and the process view of the organization. NICT offers the technical tools needed to develop management control systems that assure communication, coordination and goal congruence in the process organization.

C. Information operational and performance

The study of information use has been gaining popularity in the marketing field since the early 1980s with the recognition that it is the use, rather than the mere acquisition of information which affects organizational performance. Though the literature on information use is well developed, there is little in the way of empirical evidence concerning information use as applied to *export* decision-making.

In this field, Adamantios Diamantopoulos and Anne L. Souchon (see Chapter 5: "Information Utilization by Exporting Firms: Conceptualization, Measurement and Impact on Export Performance") propose a conceptualization of export information use, encompassing instrumental/conceptual and symbolic use of export information. Instrumental/conceptual use represents a rational way of using information in the making of current and future export decisions. On the other hand, symbolic use reflects a political use of information whereby the latter is distorted, manipulated or used for reasons other than making decisions (e.g., to justify decisions already made or to ensure good relationships with information providers). Six scales pertaining to the instrumental/conceptual and symbolic use of export marketing research, export assistance, and export market intelligence information are developed and shown to possess good reliability and validity.

Several propositions regarding the impact of export information use on export performance are tested on a sample of UK exporters. It is concluded that export information should be widely disseminated within exporting organizations in order to be used by functional areas other than the export department. Information should be used instrumentally/conceptually when it has been acquired via export market intelligence sources, however, such use should be cautious where export marketing research and export assistance information are concerned. Finally, regardless of the export information source, symbolic use should be avoided as it has a negative impact on export performance.

4.   Information systems and organizational structures

Yves De Rongé's contribution addresses the modalities of control within companies. But new information and communication technologies exercise an influence well beyond this particular aspect and relate to organizational structures as a whole. In return, organizational missions bring about alternative information architectures.

In general terms, we accept that each type of organization is characterized by specific conditions for coordination and exchange (and, therefore, different information and communication systems). A. Picot and R. Reichwald[11] have outlined

---

11   see Picot, A./Reichwald, R./Wigand, R.T. (1996): op. cit., p. 167.

the range of possibilities according to four modalities: hierarchy, market, network, and clan (see figure 1.1).

Figure 1.1: **Forms of organization and macro structures of information and communication**

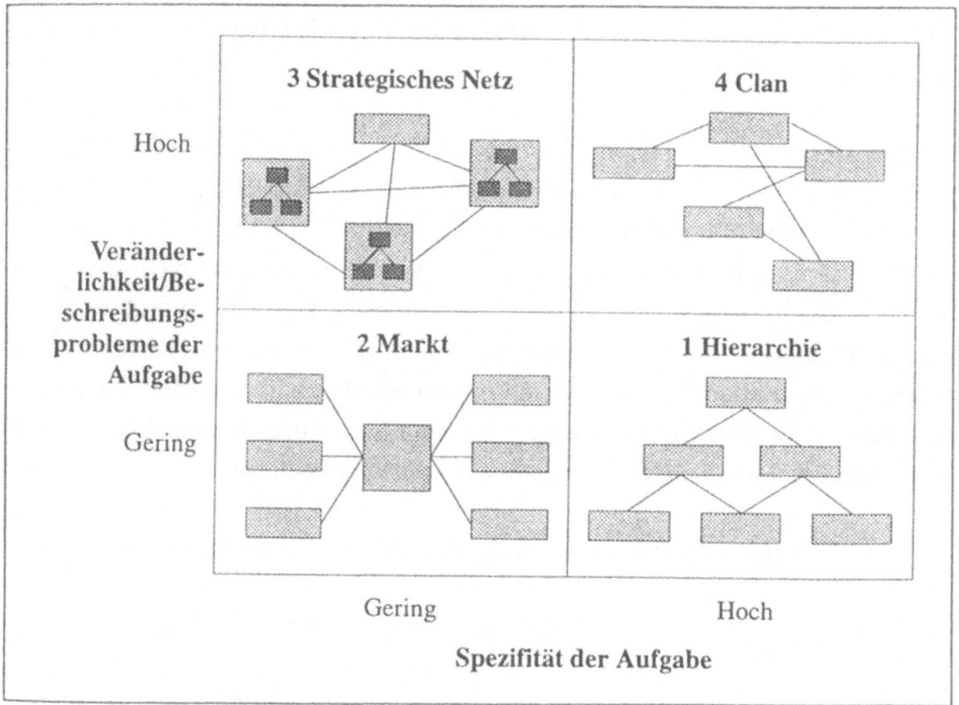

Organization and coordination structures are linked to goals on the one hand and to exchange conditions on the other. From the time that information and communication technologies are introduced, resulting in a prodigious multiplication of signals and information, the existing organizational structures are put into question and tend, furthermore to become hybridized.

The hierarchical organization has become obsolete with its unwieldy functioning modes and is too rigid in the face of globalized competition and rapid changes in technology and financing. This does not mean that the hierarchical organization does not continue to exist both in large organizations (mass production, for example) and in small organizations (specialized production, for example). The organization of information within a company generates a certain power which is used to the advantage of those who control it and are able to capitalize on their knowledge of the organization. Thus, information, power and efficiency are linked. Giovanni Palmerio analyzes these links from an Italian perspective in chapter 6 entitled "Information, Power and Efficiency: The Case of Small and Medium Size Italian Firms". In the case of Italy, the organization of companies into networks makes the analysis more difficult.

The market creates other types of relationships. Companies and consumers alike find themselves in the marketplace where they are becoming interdependent due to pricing. For a certain mode of thought (theory of general economic equilibrium), price is the only information possessed by the market participants, or exchangers. This is a questionable view; the development of the theory of information proves that producers and consumers create and utilize many pieces of information besides price. The information is neither perfect nor free, and Arrow[12] emphasizes the inequality of its distribution. Will new information technologies falsify Arrows argument of the early 1970's? Certainly not. One must make a distinction between information about the behavior of the agents which is one thing and the behavior itself which is another. Abstract, rational, routine, or real behaviors are likely to be different. These behaviors will also be impacted, or modified by electronic markets.

The problem of the quality of information and that of the deformation of information are treated here from a new angle in Chapter 7 ("The Valuation Consequences of International Joint Ventures: A Learning Perspective"). Constantinos C. Markides and Elizabeth A.M. Tracy verify the quality and

---

12 Arrow, K.J. (1974): General Economic Equilibrium Purpose, Analytic Techniques, Collective Choice, *American Economic Review*, Vol. 64, N° 3, June, pp. 253-272.

interpretation of certain pieces of information which are delivered by financial markets and related to joint ventures. More precisely, the question posed is the following: Do joint ventures (domestic and international) add value to the UK parent firms? Markides and Tracy try to answer this question by looking at shareholder benefits from the announcement of new joint ventures. Abnormal returns to shareholders are used as a measure of the stock market's *ex ante* expectations of joint venture performance. May the stock market be considered as efficient? The majority of research on financial market efficiency supports the idea that the market is informationally efficient, meaning share prices reflect all information which is publicly available and respond rapidly to new information; but biases do exist. Managers' assessments also may be inaccurate or biased.

Paolo Bertoletti (in Chapter 8, "Economic Integration Effects on Market Structure") addresses the question of information delivered by imperfect markets (with differentiated products and increasing returns to scale). Whatever the theoretical models of analysis, managers have to make decisions with increasingly imperfect information, given the complexity of the environment.

Hans Abele, in Chapter 9 "Asymmetric Information as a Problem for Financing Small or Medium Size Enterprises", examines, the role of information in the decision-making process and in the development of certain activities. If information reduces uncertainty and creates confidence, we can conversely state that the lack of information creates problems. We must, then, begin to correct the asymmetry because the need for information is growing. On the other hand, we must find solutions for the current economic challenges. Credibility and performance within an organization go hand in hand.

5.   Conclusion

In conclusion, we can affirm that new information and communication technologies offer players an exceptional opportunity to correct previous imperfections and lacunas. So long as these systems are correctly mastered (with the creation of adequate information systems and the intelligent utilization of networks), these information technologies have an exceptional potential for performance improvements. The range of their application is general; it covers all areas of a company: research and development, procurement, production, logistics, marketing, sales, and related services. These new information and communication technologies will also have an impact on all areas of competitiveness: saving of resources, cost reduction, productivity, organizational flexibility, risk reduction (and, therefore, price reduction), matching of products to demand, quantitative and qualitative development of services, and stimulation of creativity. More frequent (and better) flows of information may be exchanged in good conditions, facilitate regulation and coordination of activities, stimulate and rationally manage partnership activities, and react to the new needs of communication in a split society. However, these positive results will not be achieved unless efforts in training, and the integration of these new tools into existing mental and organizational structures, match the considerable technological changes that are taking place.

Sabine URBAN and Constantin NANOPOULOS

Résumé

Information et management : une évolution radicale

Ce chapitre présente le contenu de l'ouvrage en reliant les différents thèmes traités à la problématique générale des changements organisationnels induits par les "nouvelles technologies de l'information et de la communication". L'avenir se présente avec un certain nombre de mutations qui touchent en premier lieu le secteur d'activité de l'information et de la communication lui-même. Ce sont ensuite des utilisations de ces technologies informationnelles qui viennent modifier les processus de gestion, que ce soit au niveau de la stratégie de développement des entreprises, au niveau des opérations fonctionnelles ou de l'organisation du contrôle. Ce sont enfin les structures organisationnelles existantes (marché, hiérarchie, réseau, clan) qui sont touchées.

Zusammenfassung

Information und Management : eine radikale Entwicklung

In diesem Kapitel wird der Inhalt des gesamten Buches zusammengefaßt, indem die behandelten Themen mit der allgemeinen Problematik des durch die neuen Informations- und Kommunikationstechnologien ausgelösten Organisationswandels in Verbindung gebracht werden. Eine Reihe weiterer, vorrangig den Informations- und Kommunikationssektor berührender Veränderungen ist in Zukunft zu erwarten. Der Einsatz dieser Informationstechnologien wird die Managementprozesse verändern, sei es im Bereich der Entwicklung der Unternehmensstrategien, sei es auf der Ebene des operativen Geschäfts oder des Controlling. Schließlich sind auch die Organisationsstrukturen (Markt, Hierarchie, Netze, Clans) betroffen.

References

ARROW, K.J. (1974): General Economic Equilibrium Purpose, Analytic Techniques, Collective Choice. *American Economic Review*. Vol. 64. N° 3. Juin. pp. 253-272.

BARNEY, J.B./OUCHI, W.G. (Ed.) (1988): *Organizational Economies; Toward a New Paradigm for Understanding and Studying Organizations*. Jossey-Bass Publ. San Francisco.

BENIGER, J.R. (1986): *The Control Revolution; Technical and Economic Origins of the Information Society*. Harvard University Press. Cambridge MA.

EVANS, P.B./WURSTER, T. (1997): Strategy and the New Economics of Information. *Harvard Business Review*. Sept.-Oct. pp. 71-82.

FORRESTER, J.W. (1961): *Industrial Dynamics*. Wiley. New-York.

GADDIS, P.O. (1997): Strategy under Attack. *Long Range Planning*. Vol. 30. N° 1. pp. 38-45.

KOENIG, G. (1990): *Management stratégique ; Vision, manoeuvres et tactiques*. Nathan. Paris.

MEADOWS, D. and D./RANDERS, J./BEHRENS, W. (1972): *The Limits to Growth*. Massachussets Institute of Technology (MIT). Boston.

MINTZBERG, H. (1994): *The Rise and Fall of Strategic Planning*. The Free Press. New-York.

OCDE (1997): *Perspectives de technologies de l'information*. Paris ; *L'Observateur de l'OCDE*. N° 206. Juin-Juillet.

PICOT, A./REICHWALD, R./WIGAND, R. (1996): *Die grenzenlose Unternehmung ; Information, Organisation und Management*. Gabler. Wiesbaden.

REIX, R. (1995): *Systèmes d'information et management des organisations*. Vuibert. Paris.

ZECKHAUSER, R.J./KEENEY, R.L./SEBENIUS, J.K. (1996): *Wise Choices ; Decisions, Games and Negotiations*. Harvard Business School Press. Boston.

Constantin Nanopoulos

The Future Changes in Statistical Record Keeping

1.   Introduction

2.   Record keeping
      A. The activity
      B. The actors
      C. The roles
      D. Statistical record keeping

3.   Evolution in the factors influencing future developments in RK
      A. Technological trends and RK
      B. The evolution of ethics
      C. Changes in the organisation of international systems

4.   Changes in administrative records
      A. Central systems
      B. Regional and local systems
      C. Complex distributed organisations

5.   Trends in business record keeping
      A. Globalisation effects
      B. Effects on business information systems

6.   Trends in household's record keeping

7. Expected changes in statistical record keeping
   A. Registers
   B. Data structures
   C. Methodology
   D. Changes in the collection of data
   E. Changes in the storage of data
   F. Knowledge treatment and data analysis
   G. Dissemination
   H. Confidentiality

8. Changes in the contents. The user needs

9. Challenges for the official statistical systems
   A. A new role
   B. Competition from the private sector
   C. Handling information concepts and values. Flexibility - Adaptability
   D. Be able to find the necessary investment
   E. Follow-up of users' needs

1. Introduction

Approaching the 21st century we are driven by two main forces: technological progress, especially in the field of information and communication technologies (ICT), and the reorganisation of the world around new global approaches, linked to the liberalisation of the economy, environmental concerns, and health and nutrition problem, which are generating profound transformations in our societies.

"Technological and economic progress are inseparably interdependent. By sharply reducing the costs of transport and communication, technology also created the conditions for internationalisation, the process in which economies are becoming increasingly interdependent" (Scanning the future [14]). Globalisation is the new term for expressing the geographical extension of economic action, organisation of production, and market competition.

Statistics have an ever more important role to play in a world where *anticipation* and *real time decision* making will be the forces conducting demand. Record keeping (RK) as a central activity of official statistics will certainly be transformed in its contents, its means and perhaps also its goals, as new technologies will transform our societies, our ways of treating knowledge, and our ways of communicating.

The aim of this paper is to see how the activity of record keeping will change, and how its various components such as *data collection, treatment* and *dissemination* will be accomplished in the future. Certainly our interest is directed towards statistical record keeping. However, we should keep in mind that what distinguishes "statistical data" from other kinds of data is not the nature or the significance of the data but the purpose for which they are used. Any record keeping activity has a statistical content, and in this sense attention has to be also given to the evolution of record keeping in administrations, businesses and even households.

Predicting the future has always been a speculative activity even in the sciences. In our case, dependence on the rapidly changing technological context is doublefold since, it changes both means and the subject matter. Therefore speaking about future changes in a perspective larger than ten years is hazardous and may sound more like a science fiction novel.

2.   Record keeping

A.   The activity

Record keeping is the activity of systematic collection and registration of facts under pre-defined semantics and methods. In any record keeping activity there is a purpose that determines and governs this activity.

Record keeping is an extremely old human activity, having its roots in the Ancient World. It has followed the evolution of our civilisation and has been one of its basic characteristics. It determines in large part how it is organised, and how an important cross section of society's collective consciousness is handed down.

B.   The actors

Potentially all *persons*, all *companies*, all *administrations* are record keepers with statistical content and in this respect we have to focus our interest on their future attitudes and evolution in relation to the content of their records, on the means they use and the purposes they have in keeping records.

- "Public Administrations" are the biggest and most complex record keepers. Collection and archiving of information is an important and traditional activity for them, which in many cases is their principle task. They keep all kinds of records such as birth forms, census results, tax declarations, educational performance, pollution levels, etc., concerning the life of individuals, house-holds and companies, using all kinds of means, from paper files to computer records. The purposes they have are also very different: decision making, control, research, financial contributions, market analysis, are only a few out of many.

- "Companies" keep records either for their own managerial needs or because they have to provide information to the outside world. Different information systems like analytical accounts, production, human resources, commercial relations, general accounts, fiscal declarations, social security declarations, etc., are daily accumulating large masses of information most of which has statistical value.

- "Households" may also be considered as record keepers not only because they often carry out some productive activity which obliges them to keep records, but mostly because new technologies have already been introduced into the households and in the future many operations will be done through computers.

C.   The roles

In any record keeping activity we distinguish a certain number of common functionalities independent of the actor's nature and purpose. These functionalities, or roles of the actors, may be played completely or partially by the same authority or delegated to somebody else. The basic common roles are those of:

a) *The producer* is the one who decides upon and finances the activity. He determines the *purpose* and the conditions under which information will be produced. Usually all the actors are also producers for their own needs and their objective is not dissemination. This is mainly the role of National Statistical Institutes (NSI) or other similar agencies or governmental services. In the market-oriented and profit-making sector many private firms are into the business of collecting information and RK services.

b) *The provider* is the one who provides the information, most of the time on a compulsory basis. In some cases this is done on a voluntary basis, though rarely is he compensated or paid for giving the information. The main problem for providers is the burden of responding, which in many cases is significant and excessive. The typical situation is when firms have to provide very similar (though not exactly the same) information separately to several administrations. For firms, the problem arises when they have to respond to questions that cannot be easily answered from their own information systems. The provider will have to put together the information to the collector as it is in its own information systems.

c) *The collector* collects information from various providers. He has to know the providers well and be able to communicate with them. All the actors mentioned are collectors to a greater or lesser degree, some of them are primary in the sense that they collect the information directly from the providers, others are secondary as they obtain the information from other collectors.

d) *The user* is frequently the same as the collector and the producer. In the statistical RK activity the users are governmental and similar organisations, professional associations and unions, market analysts and journalists, research institutes and academics as well as single firms and even individuals.

D.   Statistical record keeping

Among the record keepers, statisticians are those collecting information on individual units for the general purpose of drawing conclusions about the whole population and not about the units. So it is the purpose that distinguishes the statistical use of the information from the other uses which are more concerned with the performance or attitudes of the individual units. This said, it is obvious that future developments of any record keeping activity having the potentiality of statistical usefulness fall within the scope of this paper. As organisation of statistical record keeping differs among countries, we will use the generic term "National Statistical Systems" and by extension we will refer to "International Statistical Systems" for the organisation of statistical record keeping at regional and international level.

3. Evolution in the factors influencing future developments in RK

A. Technological trends and RK

Certainly technological evolution is the motor of all kinds of changes in our world, as it allows the reorganisation of the economy, the remodelling of the social relations and the way of life of citizens. The Big-Bang of ICT has started and we are witnessing the first seconds of an explosion which will create a new universe on earth, an "Information" planet.

As can be observed in the latest report of the European Information Technology Observatory (see [8]) several technologies have now reached the stage where their application will deeply change our lives. Computers have grown so powerful and cost-effective that they can be found involved in a huge number of human activities all over the world.

In the US, President Clinton has launched a large programme to create the "information super-highways" that should bring the United States fully into the information age. The National Information Infrastructure (NII) is in three parts:
- the "information super-highways" initiative aimied at connecting ministries, public agencies, business, universities, hospitals, libraries and schools;
- the High Performance Computing and Networking (HPCN) programme for the development of new applications in major social fields such as health, education, traffic, management and control;
- a programme for the modernisation of public administrations and public access to information.

Similar actions are being undertaken in Europe with the launch of three types of networks:
- trans-European networks between administrations;
- a European Integrated Services Digital Network (ISDN) devised as the successor of the telephone network;

- broadband telecommunications networks to meet emerging requirements and pave the way to future telecommunications service networks.

In Japan continuation of the efforts in the ICT field in the last decade has been through the new programme for Japan's economic recovery, where several measures are planned to promote the use of ICT in major social fields and in ministries and other public services.

The ways ICT technologies will influence RK activities are manfold and they will have direct and indirect impacts. The main aspects that will most influence RK are:
- Super computers
- Telecommunications
- Information Management Intelligent Systems

a) Super Computers

The super computers available today in experimental laboratory forms will be the tools of record keeping for tomorrow. High clock speeds of more than 400 MHz and peak speeds of 6 gigaflops (10^9-floating point operations per second) with parallel processors will be able to handle and manipulate objects of high enough complexity to cover the majority of demanding statistical uses.

Powerful desktop computers based on new chips - such as the Pentium and the Power PC - make it possible to provide every user with the local power they need.

Multi-task operating systems like Windows NT, Unix and OS/2 offer access to remote, shared resources such as printers and databases. Once plugged into the emerging 'information highways', the desktop computer becomes a 'window' on the IT world ([17]).

Current research in semi-conductors, like alloys of silicon and germanium, ([16]), can form the basis of exceptionally high speed transistors.

The computers of the 21st century will come in a variety of sizes, forms, and specialisations,and will be deployed in huge numbers. After the conventional portables come "personal digital assistants", and further ahead, computers which will act like intelligent sheets of paper spread on our tables.

Yard-size displays will serve a number of purposes: video screens for home use, bulletin boards, white boards. The active badge will be a computer communicating radio which will provide to the wearer a number of services: automatically opening doors, automatic telephone forwarding, and computer displays customised for each person reading them.

b) Telecommunications

The key technologies for the developments in telecommunications are high-speed networks, cordless systems and satellites.

The wireless component of the global net will bear some resemblance to a cellular telephone network. Computers carried in trucks, ships or briefcases will be able to maintain connections and send and receive data wherever they go. Local Area Networks and Wide Area Networks will respond to the needs of service and functionality of the users. The Global Networks will allow for the communication of all kinds of information at low costs. Collection and dissemination of data will be done in a few seconds around the world. Once a language and a set of conventions have been chosen, multiplex technologies will connect virtually all computers. Information can be transmitted to one, to a subset, or to all recipients.

Certainly communication costs have to fall in order to reach a full exploitation of the systems. In a survey conducted by Reuters in Europe and US in 1993, the company found that the annual bill from European Post and Telecommunication Offices for 18 inter-European circuits came to £634,000. Calculating the price of an equivalent network in the US on a link by link, cost per mile basis, Reuters found that AT&T would charge just £62,000.

c) Information Management Intelligent Systems

In a continuous and interactive way, data structures and users needs have evolved together. From simple flat files managed with general purpose programming languages, technology went to the more sophisticated structures used by relational and object oriented data bases, spread sheets and hypertext which are managed with specialised software such as Data Base Management systems; word processors and hypertexts generators; and in the last twenty years artificial intelligence languages like LISP and PROLOG and the development of expert systems for knowledge manipulation.

The emerging new infrastructure promises to open the door to many new applications. Intelligent agent software which can scan a network of databases, full-motion video, which can bring TV to the desktop computer, and neural networks which can unravel complex data input, promise to extend the boundaries of IT.

While the new infrastructure makes many novel applications possible, it also creates *a new set of problems*. Distributing computer power is not enough. IT must also distribute *functionality*. This demands different approaches to building IT systems and the software which makes them work. Most important of all, IT systems must be tied closely to business needs. Computer users are no longer satisfied with expensive systems which only bring limited benefits. They want systems that are adaptable and can cope with changes in the way their business is organised and administered. "Two features are essential to the development of the infrastructure needed by the information society: one is a seamless interconnection of networks and the other that the services and applications which build on them should be able to work together (interoperability)" ([18] p. 13).

B.   The evolution of ethics

a) Threats to privacy from technologies
Most of the time when a person interacts with his exterior world, his act is recorded. Telephone calls, ticket reservations, tax payments, are examples of individual information normally stored in computers. The purchase of goods and services with electronic cards allow for the recording of individual information, with very strong implications for privacy. Theoretically the very same technological achievements that allows for the IT revolution are becoming a threat to the *privacy* of persons and companies. Super computers supplied

with good algorithms can find a password in a few seconds. Networks may allow access to various data bases and thus link together dispersed information about an individual. Thus some intruder can link the various records to obtain an overall picture of a person's life.

b) The legislation
People are more and more concerned about such problems, and legislators are establishing rules on data protection that affect RK attitudes and procedures. Most countries are moving towards more and more severe legislation on *privacy rights*. The European Union is on the point of adopting a special directive in this field. The Council of Europe is preparing a recommendation more specific to statistical record keeping. It seems that the activity of data protectors do not balance with the needs of the normal users and of an organised society. The ethics debate on the nature of public information and the balance between the needs of society for individual information and the rights of the individual for privacy, will be a central one in the "Information Societies".

c) Cryptography
A crucial problem with the management of record keeping and communicating through networks is the security and the protection of the confidentiality of information. Access to the data has to be perfectly identified and the use of passwords improved. Unfortunately password protection has many weaknesses, in part because they are often not chosen well (identification by guessing is easy) and in part because passwords are carried without special protection across the network and thus may be observed by those technically equipped to do so. One possible solution for this is *cryptography*, which has been developed extensively for military communications, and where several techniques (Symmetric key systems, Public Key Systems) with paired keys ([3]) are available. Typically a user of a public keying system will keep one key private and publicise the other. To transmit a confidential message to a recipient, the sender encrypts the message in the recipient's public key. Only the recipient can decrypt the message since the secret key is useful only for that purpose. The same technique but in reverse (secret key encryption by the

sender-public key decryption by the receiver) can be used for an electronic signature.

Fortunately IT is not only a threat to privacy. It is also a precious aid for protecting privacy, and researchers are making substantial progress in this domain. Technology is moving towards almost sure (with probability one) protection in both areas: accessing the data and understanding the data. In the area of accessing the data, technology is complementing password methods with voice recognition, finger prints recognition and other kinds of methods (see [4]). In the area of cryptography considerable progress has been made and double key methods for encrypting and decrypting the data or digital signature techniques are already available and will be improved in the future.

C.   Changes in the organisation of international systems

a) Globalisation

The "International environment is composed of more and more numerous actors struggling for power and survival" (S. Urban [6]). This brings continual instability and, a need to adapt to the new conditions. Flexibility of structures and pertinent information for immediate decision making are the weapons to not lose the battle. Production is no longer a national concept ([10]) as acquisitions, partnership, sub-contracting, etc., are the new elements of the organisation of production.

Globalisation brings in contact a diversity of *legislation*, of *norms*, of *cultures* creating new needs for information and communication and new concepts that have to be measured, challenging statisticians as some of their traditional achievements become sooner or later obsolete. To be more precise, it is not the classical tools that will be inadequate but the fact that although the phenomena and the concepts will lose their national dimensions, statistical systems will remain national and their capacities of measuring may risk being limited to events in their national territories.

b) Users' Needs: More, Faster, Better

Technological evolution is the carrier of changes in the structure of data, adapting to new expressions of the users' needs in a more efficient way. Specialisation of the structures of information is also a need in order to provide information services adapted to the users' profile. Users will keep asking for more information to be provided almost immediately and, will want it to be of excellent quality. They will need better assistance in using information, and new services will develop related to choices among various concepts, utilisation and decision preparation.

4. Changes in administrative records

A. Central systems

Administration will have to invest in new technologies in order to be able to follow the evolution of the globalisation effects and the technological investments of the firms. It would be anachronistic and practically unacceptable for them not to move into the Electronic Data Interchange (EDI) and networking communication. In fact as we have seen in §3.1 in most of the developed world the necessary investments are already in the pipeline.

In this context, an *explosion* should be expected in administrative record keeping. Business information records will have the tendency to increase, fuelled by globalisation needs and in spite of the deregulation spirit which will govern many of the developed countries economic systems. Administration records in the large economic spaces like the European Union (EU), North Atlantic Free Trade Association (NAFTA), Association of South East Asian Nations (ASEAN) and others will tend to increase and become more harmonised. Financial and trade information will increase, covering the environment, social conditions, resources and food provisions, population and migration. These will be some of the important administrative information systems which will undergo strong development in the next decades.

B.   Regional and local systems

Regional and local authorities will continue their efforts to develop local information systems for their own management and decision making. The spreading use of GISs (Geographic Information Systems) may give rise to distributed GIS interconnected through global networks. Remote sensing will produce large amounts of local information feeding the GISs ([1]).

C.   Complex distributed organisations

As the complexity of the relations and interdependencies of nations and societies will keep growing, administrative systems at national and international level will need more information reflecting those relations. New elements will be introduced in the statistical systems like, for example, those related to the relations of enterprises at the international level. Financial links, partnerships, sub contracting, and other relations will need new information concepts to be followed. The different approaches that will have to be faced by administrations will require *specialised information systems* which will have to interface between the profile of the user and the multitude of types of data. Data and meta-data will have to be organised on the basis of multilevel systems interfacing the distributed multi-source multi-location environment of the production of data with the specialised needs of the user.

The tendency in administrations is to create internal information systems from scratch coping with the specific needs of the administration. This is due to the differences of the nature of the information needed and from the costs of transforming existing information. Typically those systems are not accessible to other administrations.

New technology is an opportunity to change this situation because it has the capacity to introduce *sufficient harmonisation of concepts at a low level* to give the possibility of all kinds of aggregations. The more elementary the information is, the more useful it will be.

This implies that statisticians have to be present in all the international committees that are dealing with the harmonisation of administrative or business concepts in order to insure compatibility with statistical purposes.

Communication standards for statistics have been developed in recent years within the Message Development Group 6 of the Western European EDIFACT Board (WE/EB MD6). More has to be done for the world-wide harmonisation of the concept used within the information systems. This is the role of the many international agencies, organisations and associations, dealing directly or indirectly with the contents of records kept by the various actors.

5.   Trends in business record keeping

A.   Globalisation effects

"In order to compete globally, radical changes were introduced in the organisation of production. Production is now set up on a modular basis, whereby production of the modules is often spread out across the globe, depending on the comparative advantages of the regions" ([14]). As a result many corporations now function within a *global network*, which has resulted in new forms of internationalisation, the so-called "intra-firm trade" which already constitutes an important part of international trade.

B.   Effects on business information systems

a) Business accounts
The globalisation of the economy and the new organisation of business at world level, the European single market, NAFTA, World Trade Organisation (WTO),... are transforming the structures and relations of enterprises. New concepts are continuously created, progressively transforming the systems of business accounts. Partnerships in public procurements, subcontracting, human resources, technological resources (patents, designs, trade marks, name),

investment, currency provisions, risk management and many others are indicative elements of changing business information systems.

Every developed country has imposed statutory book keeping to be maintained by companies. In Europe some countries require books of accounts or the equivalent for the purpose of maintaining adequate records. In other countries the requirements are within "Accounting Plans". The accounting standards range from "pragmatic" in the UK, through the principles of "good keeping" and "orderly keeping" in the Netherlands and Germany to the strict requirements of the plans in France, Belgium, Greece, Portugal and Spain ([15]).

b) Future development

As new technologies and international needs will reinforce standardisation in business information systems it will be easier for national and international administration to obtain informations.

At the same time the establishment at international level of professionally qualified and experienced auditors and of new units, like the "European Company" and the "European Interest Group" will progressively create an "international accounting plan" for companies.

The main areas of harmonisation relevant to accounting systems are:
– Company law
– Laws relating to professions
– Law relating to stock exchanges and securities
– Law relating to banks and credit institutions
– Taxation laws
– Law relating to consumer prices

(A detailed presentation of these topics may be found in: "Accounting systems and practices in Europe" ([13])).

An acceptable development will be the harmonisation of the "analytical business accounting systems" around a few standards through commercial software as this is a "free" area for standardisation as opposed to those more closely "administered" by national authorities declarative systems.

In small companies, every function is often managed by different software (accounting, invoicing, salaries...), and the connection between all these different packages is complex, even sometimes impossible. In this case data extraction for statistical purposes is quite difficult, and often the data has to be taken from other sources. The situation is quite different in the big enterprises. There is often a single piece of software that manages all the firm's functions, which given appropriate coding, enable it to produce needed statistical data much easier.

Integration of the various information systems will be the future for all companies, small and large, giving them the same opportunities for effective communication and management. This will be achieved only if there is an interoperability of systems. The first step in that direction is the pre-harmonisation of the basic concepts used at enterprise level. "The business economist and others concerned about the quality of government data should work with accountants, controllers, and others in the company to make sure that the internal data are in order and that government forms submitted provide an accurate picture and a sound estimate of the information being requested ([2] p. 42).

6.   Trends in household's record keeping

Today hundreds of millions of households are equipped with personal computers which are used mostly for educational purposes, entertainment, communications, word-processing and small data bases. Initially, cost and lack of education slowed down this market. As PCs became cheaper and individuals more computer literate, the PC market took off and many programmes appeared catering to household record keeping.

Research and standardisation for the development of intelligent personal health cards will allow individuals to carry with them, just like any other credit card in their wallet, all the information about their health. Similar intelligent cards will be developed for money transfer.

As Prof. Michael Dertouzos from MIT (see [5]), envisions it, "Consumers would broadcast (electronically) their needs to suppliers, creating a kind of reverse advertising. Many goods would be ordered and paid electronically. A parent could deliver work to a physically distant employer while taking care of children at home...".

Many of these things are already available for the initiated and well equipped (computer and modem, or minitel in France) consumer. It is the generalisation that will take place in the future. Households will be more systematic record keepers as new tools are introduced into houses. Hopefully many statistical applications will take advantage of records, as it will be possible to collect statistics on household behaviour more quickly and more cheaply than current methods.

7.   Expected changes in statistical record keeping

Record keeping for statistical purposes will keep changing in a continuity background. Probably within twenty five years everything will be different from today. Lets not forget that the paper is about *expected* changes, not unexpected.

A.   Registers

Registers are the fundamental tools for record keeping as they identify the units concerned: they follow their evolution, they can verify their relation with the collector and they allow the *linkage* of information among different producers and collectors. New technologies will improve the quality of the registers as their updating will no longer be a problem, even for very small enterprises which are usually the difficult customers of a statistical business register. Other types of registers for buildings and houses, cars, ships, etc. will improve their quality and their communications capabilities.

The effects of globalisation will be statistically measurable only if the reconstitution of the elements from different countries is be possible by the communication of different registers at international level. This is a difficult task, not from the technical point of view, which will not be a problem, but from the *administrative* aspect, as most national legislation does not allow linkage of registers with those of other countries.

B. Data structures

a) Multi-media

Technological evolution as described above will create more and more specific data structures to fulfil particular user needs. As data types are extended to images, sounds and knowledge, and as utilisation involves multimedia technologies, data structures will be adapted to incorporate these new types and the manipulation of this data could become even more complex for the user. This difficulty will be overcome by the development of specialised intelligent software which will replace current data base management systems, whilst always moving towards more and more natural user language systems.

Multi-media objects, knowledge data and virtuality will be the elements which will meet the large variety of needs. Integration of "objects" into the statistical data base will allow for new data representations which will enhance the presentation of the conclusions in statistical analysis.

b) Meta Data

Meta data will link more and more distributed specialised information systems like today geographical co-ordinates may link various information entities with some spatial reference. Statistical Meta Information systems of global or local scope (see [9]) are examples of new data structures which are under investigation and which will change the nature of statisticians' work in the future.

C. Methodology

Methodology is firmly linked to the purpose of the RK activity. It determines the semantic content of the information, the methods and tools of the collection and dissemination of the data. It needs theoretical and scientific knowledge of the phenomena, practical knowledge about the organisation of the units of observation, and administrative capacity to make the appropriate choices. The evolution of this activity depends on the evolution of the needs of the users, as far as the content of the statistical systems is concerned, but the new future phenomenon is that methodology will depend on the technology too as artificial intelligence techniques will come to help in this domain.

a) Intelligent management
Methodology is traditionally a paper-based activity, which will have to change dramatically in the future as increasing globalisation creates new concepts, and the needs for harmonisation at world level becomes more apparent. Techno-logical achievements will allow the creation of intelligent systems for the management of methodological knowledge and the co-ordination of various domains. It is very probable than within five or ten years, we will be equipped with *methodological expert* systems able to assist producers and users of statistical information in a multilingual environment.

b) Statistical units
The basic element of the RK activity is the record unit. This is the elementary reference of the collected information and determines the possibilities offered for mixing and aggregation and creation of new records. There is a hierarchical relation in most units for example between local unit/enterprise/group or between local unit/region/country or between person/household/region, etc. Globalisation will certainly affect the concepts used and the relations between statistical units used in business surveys. As we have already indicated, the European Union has created two trans-national concepts, the "European Company" and the "European Economic Interest Group".

c) Classifications

An important change that may be expected is in the area of classifications. So far they have been dinosaurs; difficult to change and obsolete by the time they have been agreed. On a rapidly changing world will need much faster adaptation of classifications. A way of achieving that is automatic classification techniques constructed directly from the information available on the units in statistical registers.

D.   Changes in the collection of data

a) Collection techniques will depend on the development of networks and super computers which will offer all kinds of possibilities for data collection from all three actors. New legislation is expected to be less easily available for compulsory data collection, thus limiting the possibilities for statistics. On the other hand, as the needs for information increase and individual information has more market value, it is possible that collectors may find it financially viable to pay providers.

Collection may be done just by administrative procedures or, it may also need scientific skills for the organisation of the operations. The most important aspect is *the means and the tools used* for the collection of the information. This has been subject to tremendous changes in the second half of this century and more important changes are expected in the near future. Communication networks, access to administrative records, development of statistical provider oriented information systems, and remote sensing are the most important issues for the future developments of this component.

Currently data collection is facing three problems: administrative costs, response burden, ethical attitudes. Certainly ICT technologies offer potential solutions to these problems, but those solutions cannot be achieved without prior investment at the NSI and at the providers levels. The providers are not going to invest in ICT just to be able to respond to statistical demands. Statistical response will be a by-product of the computerisation of companies and households for their own existing needs. We believe that within the next ten years all firms, including even the smallest ones, will have reached an appropriate level of computerisation and networking so that they will be able to provide and receive statistical information and meta-information at low cost. For this to happen we have to pave the technological and conceptual way between business information systems and statistical information systems. This is the objective of the SERT-BISE project of Eurostat. A project under development for the use of telematics to exchange (statistical) data between firms and administrations (SERT = Statistique d'Entreprises et Réseaux Télématiques, BISE = Base d'Information Statistique de l'Entreprise).

Communicating with tens or hundreds of thousands of providers through networks is the new challenge for the NSI. This needs standards, rules, equipment, and knowledge which in other words means methodology, legislation, investment, and training. Several EU countries have already taken initiatives in data collection with EDI techniques. A recent study from Eurostat ([12]) done within the SERT project has reported on many of these initiatives (EDISTAT in Germany, EDIFIEE in France, etc.) taken by NSIs, often in cooperation with business associations, showing that statisticians are working towards the tools for tomorrow's data collection.

b) The Intrastat paradigm

An example of an important change in well established statistical systems which took place recently in Europe is the case of Intrastat. After the realisation of the single market, trade statistics between the twelve member states were no longer collected by means of customs declarations. Reporting is now done directly to the NSI by the firms. In order to facilitate the task for the firms, EDI techniques have been developed for filling the forms and transmitting the results on diskette. Thus the overall burden to the information provider has been reduced whilst still collecting adequate information on intra EC trade.

E. Changes in the storage of data

Storage capacities will increase giving the possibility of having huge data quantities on one site, but at the same time the development of networks and the super computers will offer all kinds of possibilities for distributed data storage, which will usually be completely transparent to the user. Both systems will coexist as potential options to the producer, who will have to decide on the basis of cost-efficiency criteria.

NSIs will probably continue to maintain a centralised data service, to meet the needs of large scale data treatment and dissemination. Nevertheless the multiplication of data sources will create a problem of running and controlling geographically distributed large heterogeneous data bases which will be solved with the development of Distributed Database Management Systems ([11]). Access by customers to statistical databases with data and meta data can be efficiently done if the NSIs develop distributed customer oriented databases.

F.   Knowledge treatment and data analysis

This is a key area for enhancing the producer's added value. The capacity for transforming information from one level reference system to the next level reference system will be at the heart of a high performance information service. The process followed going from the data collection to the final use of the relevant information for a binary decision is like a set of successive transformations which, in an injective way, step by step transforms information from one reference level to another. It is the analogue to the transformation of hundreds of thousands of prices of particular products into price indexes for a particular sector in a particular region and then by aggregation for a country, continuing to more aggregate levels.

Transformation of the information to a user specific reference system will be essential for future statistical systems to be competitive.

G. Dissemination

It will be possible to disseminate statistics to a much wider audience in the future, as *networks* will directly connect users and the producers. Entering the era of global networks by the end of this century, our market will be the whole world. Offering toll-free access to our product catalogues, we should be able to receive orders and prepare specialised customer oriented products.

Of course networks will not be the only means of dissemination. Limitation of the number of connections and costs will allow for parallel ways. Not that the beauty of paper publications will disappear from our bookshelves as a persistent romanticism will continue to have numerous followers, but new media like *CD-ROMs*, already in use, will offer many advantages for utilisation, storage capacities, consultation facilities, transportability, etc. The evolution of the cheap writable optical disk will certainly give the possibility to the NSI to propose personalised CDs on demand together with more general customer products.

Manual data capture will largely be phased out within the next two decades. Already code-bar systems together with optical electronic recognition and voice recognition are replacing old keypunching machines. Proliferation of data together with the expansion of data structures will lead statisticians into the manipulation of *Very Large Data Systems* (VLDS) using super computers and distributed architectures within networks. An example may be the use of parallel processing in order to handle simultaneously the data and the meta-data, or using a Geographic information system for Transport to draw the corresponding map of CO_2 emissions by cars. This will need to work simultaneously with Transport, Energy and cartography data-bases. Very detailed data will certainly be available but dispersed in many locations and the problem will be to orchestrate communications between all these systems.

Timeliness will be a synonym for "now". As control and decision making will tend to be on a real time basis, information systems will tend to be updated on a real time basis also.

It is not impossible that statistical time periods will be adjusted to the periods used by firms and administrations for the creation of the information. Taking Foreign Trade activities as an example, we observe that the companies operate at "transaction level" and they have information at "order" level. The order form contains a lot of information that can be taken as a basis for many information systems: Market analysis, Statistical declarations etc. We can imagine that we will be able to collect information on a more detailed level than statisticians are doing now - more detailed nomenclatures, more detail on destination, packaging forms, transportation means etc. Who can do more can do less...

H.   Confidentiality

Confidentiality as a central concern in statistical record keeping is largely affected by the information technologies and as it was pointed out in §3.2 more legislation for data protection is expected in the future.

There is a danger that data protection legislation may have negative effects on statistical RK activities because it will give less access to the primary sources, fewer possibilities in archiving and accessing archives, and fewer possibilities for data dissemination. It may make, access to administrative sources difficult. This danger has been foreseen by the DGINS of the EU countries which have proposed a special community regulation on the transmission of confidential data from the NSI to Eurostat, and they are following the legislative work at the EU level closely.

8.   Changes in the contents. The user needs

We already stressed the fact that the new organisation of the world will develop new concepts and new needs that will change considerably the contents of the statistical information systems at least in some areas. New technologies will offer not only the "syntax" for the communication of data, but will also offer the possibility of treating the "semantics". The combination of these two concepts will create the future "statistical information objects".

a) Services

The "Services" area is still in its infancy with a lot of difficulties in producing quality information. Official statistics has lagged behind the economic and organisational reality in this field, and there is a great danger that the gap is going to increase as the "services structures" are subject to rapid evolution. The "information society" is going to need more information on information. Certainly the tools at our disposal today, such as activity and product nomenclatures or registers and statistical units, are not appropriate for an adequate approach to services phenomena because they have been forged to serve national purposes in a manufacture based economy.

b) Social statistics

Demographic projections of the United Nations ring alarm bells for extreme pressure on the economies of Less Developed Countries (LDCs), which in combination with existing differences in prosperity will cause migratory movements to the Developed Countries (DCs). The new multi-cultural social environments and the fragility of the social systems in DCs will certainly increase demand for social statistics. As well as classical population, unemployment and employment related statistics, new domains are even now under development in the national and international statistical system, such as social security, housing, accidents, ageing, family, etc.

c) Environmental Statistics

The international concern on environmental issues has already considerably increased the need for information at regional, national and international levels. As human activities from the past and present create pollution problems, information systems have to be set up in order to follow and monitor these phenomena. Ground water pollution and its links to specific activities like agriculture and industry demand topological relations, locally and at a continental level. The same is true for air pollution from the emissions of industry, transport, and residential heating.

In the report (see [7]) of the European Union's panel No. 9 on Environment Telematics, the panel stresses the need for setting up new data collection systems within the CORINE (Coordination d'Information Environnementale) programme. Pre-harmonisation should be a concern in this area.

9.   Challenges for the official statistical systems

A.   A new role

The evolution foreseen in the previous paragraphs will have important consequences for official statistical systems as they indicate the possibilities for important developments allowing optimists to dream of a "golden era of official statistics", but at the same time they reveal important threats that permit pessimists to ring alarm bells for official statistics. It is true though that most of the foreseen changes are major challenges to the statisticians, who will in the future have to fight to remain relevant.

In this new data market, the role of the statistician will be changed. He will continue to have to check the validity of the data, to transcode it and to make sense out of it. As these data will be widely available, he will have to propose conceptual frameworks which will make it possible to integrate in a coherent way the existing pieces of information. He will be asked to judge the relevance of conclusions based on specific data, to balance evidence. His role will partly switch from a data collector, to an information extractor and maybe in some cases a referee. He will have to educate, to model.

B.   Competition from the private sector

Probably in the future the number of collectors/producers will increase, especially within the private sector, and public collectors will have to compete with them, as in many countries the attitude towards the statistical services is pushing them to work on a more competitive basis. This certainly is going to be a major challenge for many of the NSIs.

As information tends to be more and a more a market product, we will have to better define its value. The providers may ask for payment in return of information.

Raw information will be like raw materials. The ones who can transform it into the best products will win in the market competition. Certainly after the full development of networks and standards, we will witness a proliferation of collectors and disseminators of information services. Being quick, fast, and pertinent will be the characteristics of the competition. As I have already pointed out, I believe that high performance systems will develop for market oriented services which will include statistics. It will be easy for a private firm to choose a sample of firms from a list of network customers and ask them to supply, on a confidential and contractual basis, detailed information in return for payment, and to set up longitudinal follow-up surveys of performances, market opportunities, product evolution, forecasts etc... All this information might be collected within a few hours, then processed and combined with other information, and sent via networks to customers.

Statistical agencies, like many other administrations, do not keep analytical accounts and thus, cannot analyse the costs of their products. In the future they will probably have to move in this direction because due to competition, costs and prices will have to be followed closely.

C.   Handling information concepts and values. Flexibility - Adaptability

The existing data will serve different administrative or technical purposes. They will probably be exchanged and stored according to international and agreed standards. The content will be heterogeneous. However the need for concept harmonisation will rapidly appear and the statistical use, by linking these different sources, will make some type of harmonisation indispensable. More and more, the statistician will have his say in the design of information systems.

As information proliferates and is easily available to many users, the problems of harmonisation will be crucial, especially to those handling multinational sources. Although standardisation will be higher for the concepts belonging to the same information systems, e.g. exchange of information between *companies*, there is a danger that similar concepts in different systems will not coincide. In an extremely fast moving world with an explosion of information concepts, the role of statistical RK will take more of a reference value.

Certain statisticians argue that as structures are changing so rapidly, there is no point in trying to follow an ever changing system. I believe they are wrong in the sense that our professional objective is to reflect the evolution of society, and thus if socio-economic systems are changing, statistical systems have to be adapted. Think of the future revolution in information services. In the next two decades, scientists are promising spectacular changes. Are our systems able to follow and report on these changes? Not for the moment, because the means we have today are not adapted for following such rapid changes. This has to do with the fact that most of the collection is done on paper questionnaires implying large resources for the collection and storage at the administration level and important burdens on the respondents. I hope and strongly believe that technology is going to solve these current problems and in the future we will have to work differently.

D.   Be able to find the necessary investment

As technologies keep changing so rapidly, investment will be needed to follow them up and to remain competitive with the private sector, which certainly will move into RK activity with new ambitions and more flexible financial constraints. Will NSIs have to move into market competition? This is very plausible, unless a change in the political climate continues to insure exclusivity of official sources. In any case the challenge for NSIs will be to convince their public authorities that they have to make the new investments needed in the next five to ten years by proving on the basis of cost-benefit analysis the advantages of doing so.

In order to succeed in this accounting operation we have to understand better the cost of a statistical action. Costs to the administration for creating and maintaining the system, costs to the respondents for providing the information, collection costs, etc.

Anticipation of the future needs and estimation of the costs in alternative situations will also be additional elements in their evaluations.

E.   Follow-up of users' needs

As competition grows and the users' needs become more diverse, knowledge of the market will be essential to survive. This will impose pressure within the NSI to devote more resources to the investigation of the market and the follow-up of user needs. Productivity will push towards RK activities covering the maximum possible of uses. For example, data collection on production and trade of products together with production and consumption prices, may serve, through sufficiently detailed nomenclatures, for market analysis.

Production of simply figures will not be enough to fulfil users' needs for information of complex structures mixing data with other "essential" information such as meta-data.

In order to be competitive we will have to use the statistical information for as many purposes as possible in relation to the demand. An illustrative example is "forecasting", a forbidden activity for official statistics with a high demand.

Résumé

L'évolution de la gestion des informations statistiques

La gestion des informations statistiques s'applique à la collecte des données, leur traitement et leur dissémination. Au coeur de ce dispositif se situe le stockage des données statistiques et le problème de l'accès à ces informations. Le progrès technique (on utilise le sigle de NTIC pour les Nouvelles Technologies de l'Information et de la Communication) a dans ce domaine un impact considérable à la fois aux plans économique (processus et temps de la prise de décision), organisationnel et politique (réseaux de pouvoir), ainsi qu'éthique (confidentialité et usage de données individuelles).

Ce chapitre commence par présenter l'architecture des systèmes d'information : les acteurs (administrations, entreprises, particuliers), leur rôle (production, diffusion, collecte, utilisation des informations), les liens établis entre eux dans le cadre d'un système statistique national devenant international. Cette architecture subit des transformations profondes à l'heure actuelle sous l'effet d'une évolution technologique envahissante et de la globalisation de l'économie admise comme une tendance dominante inévitable. Les prétentions des utilisateurs deviennent elles aussi plus grandes : on exige des informations pertinentes, plus nombreuses, plus rapides et de qualité fiable. Comment répondre à ces exigences d'une manière satisfaisante ? Les chemins possibles et leurs enjeux sont présentées ici.

Constantin NANOPOULOS

Zusammenfassung

Die Weiterentwicklung der Verwaltung statistischer Daten

Die Datenverwaltung beschäftigt sich mit dem Sammeln der Daten, mit ihrer Verarbeitung und ihrer Verbreitung. Im Mittelpunkt steht dabei die Speicherung der Daten und der Zugang zu diesen Daten. Der technische Fortschritt - man verwendet dafür die Abkürzung NTCI (Neue Informations- und Kommunikationstechnologien) - ist in diesem Bereich von beträchtlicher Bedeutung und zwar sowohl in wirtschaftlicher Hinsicht (Entscheidungsprozeß und Dauer der Entscheidungsfindung), in organisatorischer und strategischer Hinsicht (Einflußvernetzungen) wie auch unter ethischen Aspekten bei der Verwendung persönlicher Daten.

Der vorliegende Beitrag stellt zunächst die Struktur der Informationssysteme dar, die Informationsverarbeiter (Behörden, Unternehmen, Privatpersonen), ihre jeweilige Rolle (Erstellung, Verbreitung, Sammlung, Verwendung der Informationen) und die zwischen ihnen bestehenden Verbindungen im Rahmen eines nationalen und zunehmend auch eines internationalen Statistiksystems. Diese Struktur erfährt derzeit unter dem Einfluß des technologischen Wandels und der Globalisierung tiefgreifende und als unvermeidlich geltende Veränderungen. Die Erwartungen der Nutzer werden auch größer: man fordert schnellere, zuverlässigere, zahlreichere und zutreffendere Informationen. Wie kann diesen Forderungen Rechnung getragen werden ? Die möglichen Wege und daraus folgenden Konsequenzen werden hier dargelegt.

References

BUNZEL, H. (1993): *Handling Statistical Meta-information using ISIS/UL*. Statistical Meta Information Systems Workshop. EUROSTAT. Luxembourg.[1]

CENTRAL PLANNING BUREAU (1992): *Scanning the Future*. The Netherlands. [14]

DERTOUZOS, M. (1991): *Scientific American*. September. [5]

DUNCAN, J.W./GROSS, A. (1993): *Statistics for the 21st Century, The Dun of Bradstreet Corporation*. New-York (USA). [2]

EUROPEAN COMMISSION TELEMATICS APPLICATION PROGRAMME 1994-98 (1994): *Panel 9. Environment*. June. Brussels. [7]

EUROPEAN INFORMATION TECHNOLOGY OBSERVATORY (EITO) (1994): Frankfurt. [8]

EUROSTAT-CESIA (1994): *Etude SERT*. June. [12]

FINANCIAL TIMES (1994): *A-Z of Computing*. April 26. [17]

HELLMAN, M.E. (1979): *The mathematics of public key cryptography*. Scientific American. April. pp. 25. [3]

HIGH LEVEL GROUP OF THE INFORMATION SOCIETY (1994): *Europe and the global information society*. EU. [18]

MEYERSON, B.S. (1994): *High-Speed Silicon-Germanium Electronics*. Scientific American. March. [16]

OLDHAM, K.M. (1989): *Accounting Systems and practices in Europe*. [13]

REICH, B.R. (1991): *The work of nations*. Simon & Schuster. London. [10]

SANDARELI, M.H. and al. (1993): *Metadata for Integrating Distributed and Heterogenious Statistical databases*. Statistical Meta Information Systems Workshop. EUROSTAT. Luxembourg. [11]

SCAUM, D. (1992): *Achieving Electronic Privacy*. Scientific American. August. pp. 38. [4]

SUNDGREN, B. (1993): *Statistical meta information systems*. Statistical Meta Information Systems Workshop. EUROSTAT. Luxembourg. [9]

TESLER, L.G. (1991): *Networked Computing in the 1990s*. Scientific American. September. pp. 54. [15]

URBAN, S. (1993): *Management International*. Litec. Paris. [6]

Markku Saaksjarvi

Product Platform and IT Infrastructure in Strategic Management of IT

1. Introduction

2. IT infrastructure in short
   A. IT infrastructure and capabilities
   B. Relation of IT infrastructure to business strategy

3. From product architecture to platform
   A. Emerging role of product architecture
   B. Product architecture and core competencies
   C. Product platform
   D. Product platform strategy

4. IT infrastructure as platform

5. Summary and conclusions

1.   Introduction

Recently, the terms global company and globalization have appeared in the headings of numerous books. Global companies have to customize universal products to meet local needs, they have shared decision processes and cross-organizational communication, they are highly networked or virtual and they have to manage their core competencies well.

Information technology is among the main drivers of globalization. Firstly, better utilization of information technology may offer new possibilities to manage and coordinate distributed organizations. Secondly, communication technology supports partnerships and virtual organizational forms. Thirdly, the new distributed computer-mediated environments like the World-Wide Web offer enormous potential as a global market place and common distribution channel. Recently, the role of an IT infrastructure as a solid common base of business operations of large and global companies has emerged. IT infrastructure is critical to globally competing firms, and investments to IT infrastructure are long-term commitments accounting for considerable share, often over half of the total IT budget.

IT infrastructure of a firm consists of IT components like common hardware, software, communication technology, data bases, standards, tools, etc. that provide shared services to large range of business applications. Human infrastructure components are also necessary in the creation of services. IT infrastructure should provide the shared and common foundation for future applications and services of all business units. However, corporate management may have great difficulties to make decisions concerning both funding of their IT infrastructure and evaluating its effectiveness. Even large investments in IT infrastructure may be ineffective.

The concept of product platform that evolved recently in the development of complex technological (architectural) products is very promising and could help to build a responsive IT infrastructure. The main idea of product platform is to enable effective generation of a whole product family from the same architectural core. Product platform is the reusable core of the product (design) architecture and the underlying technology. This main idea seems both interesting and relevant for the development of corporate IT infrastructure. IT infrastructure should have potential to serve several different customers (business units), and to be flexible and reusable. It should underpin competitive positioning of business initiatives such as redesigning processes, and also be a stabile base for applications to execute business processes. Recently, several researchers have devoted interest on the strategic role of corporate IT infrastructure. The usefulness of the ideas behind product platform has not been analyzed before.

We argue that IT infrastructure and product platform as strategic concepts have the same basic purpose. Therefore, the idea of product platform could help in the development of IT infrastructure and make strategic decisions more easy. We need a careful analysis of this concept and of its application to build effective IT infrastructures.

Objectives and outline of this paper
The general objective of this paper is to discuss the emerging concept of product platform and to make conclusions concerning its relevance to building effective and responsive IT infrastructures and to the strategic management of IT. We compare the above concepts carefully on the basis of our literature review and analyze the relevance.

The paper has the following structure. Chapter 2 contains a short description of IT infrastructure and infrastructure capabilities and we also discuss the relations and links of IT infrastructure to corporate strategy. In chapter 3 we discuss the role of product architecture, then the evolution of the concepts of product platform and platform strategy in the literature. In Chapter 4 we compare the main ideas of product platform and IT infrastructure, and list our arguments why companies should apply platform strategy to IT infrastructure. Finally, in chapter 5 we present our conclusions and define certain research areas.

2. It infrastructure in short

A. IT infrastructure and capabilities

According to Broadbent and Weill (1997) information technology infrastructure is the enabling base of shared IT capabilities that provide the foundation for other business systems. IT infrastructure is vitally important to companies, particularly those industries going through dynamic change, those reengineering their business processes, and those with widely dispersed operations. According to Miller et al. (1993) IT infrastructure is important for facilitating the development of global virtual corporations, virtual networks of partner companies, and virtual value chains. According to IS Analyzer (1991) it is critical to globally competing firms.

IT infrastructure of a firm consists of IT components like common hardware, software, communication technology, data bases, standards, tools, etc. that provide shared services to large range of business applications. In their empirical study of 26 international companies

Broadbent et al. (1996) identified five core IT infrastructure services common to all companies. These five were management of corporate communication network services, management of group-wide messaging services, recommendation standards for IT architecture, security services for firm-wide installations and applications, and technology advice and support services.

According to Broadbent et al. (1996) IT infrastructure capability is an important firm resource that is difficult to imitate because it is created through the fusion of technology and human skills. Key attributes of IT infrastructure capability are the extent to which it is shareable and reusable across the firm. However, in their empirical study they could not find any different patterns of IT infrastructure capabilities among firms with greater emphasis on flexibility to meet changing needs of their marketplace compared to firms with less emphasis on flexibility.

B.   Relation of IT infrastructure to business strategy

Several authors have argued for the need to link IT infrastructure and corporate strategy. Broadbent and Weill (1997) proposed a model based on business and IT maxims, which are short statements to express the synthesis of what infrastructure should coordinate across the firm. They proposed that the firm-wide infrastructure view could identify the firm's predominant view of infrastructure. The four generic views were none, utility, dependent, and enabling. According to the authors, the predominant view gives a context for decision making about funding for specific infrastructure services.

Henderson and Venkatraman (1993) noticed that though information technology had evolved from its traditional orientation of administrative support toward a more strategic role within an organization, there was still a lack of fundamental frameworks within which to understand the potential of IT for tomorrow's organizations. They argued that the inability to realize value from IT investments was due to the lack of alignment between the business and IT strategies of organizations. Strategic alignment was not an event but a process of continuous adaptation and change.

The alignment framework included two central concepts: strategic fit and functional integration. According to the model, it is important to make sure that both the external (strategic) and internal (implemented) domains were in fit together such the implementation of the strategy corresponds with the strategy itself. In the same way, the functional integration between business and IT domains has to be real. Only then is alignment effective. IT infrastructure has an important role in this adaptation.

Henderson and Venkatraman separated three important questions in the external IT domain: scope, competencies, and governance. The internal IT domain contained IS architecture, work processes, and skills. IT infrastructure formed the common base for these three sets.

Henderson and Venkatraman argued that it was really important to make this distinction between external and internal IT domains clear because managers tend to think in terms of the internal IT domain. However, as IT emerges as a critical enabler of business transformation with capabilities to deliver firm level advantages, firms should pay more attention to the external components of IT strategy. They called for the need to fit the external and internal domains also in the case of IT to make sure that the infrastructure will make implementation of the IT strategy possible.

The alignment model proposed four different strategy execution perspectives for the management. Either business strategy or IT strategy can be the dominant driver of alignment. The authors called the traditional business strategy driven perspective as "strategy execution", and the IT strategy driven as "service level" alignment perspective. According to this IT driven perspective, strategic decisions of IT infrastructure should give direction to business organization and processes, not the business strategy formulation. This is an interesting perspective, and it may be relevant specially in developing technology-push type of business applications. However, Henderson and Venkatraman pointed out that no one single perspective is universally superior mode of alignment.

3.   From product architecture to platform

A.   Emerging role of product architecture

Morris and Ferguson (1993) discussed the radical transformation of the global IT industry and argued that a new paradigm is required to explain patterns of competitive success and failure in information technology. They stated that the competitive success flows to the company that manages to establish proprietary architectural control over a broad, fast-moving, competitive space.

According to Morris and Ferguson, in the open-systems era, proprietary architectural coherence becomes even more necessary. A well-designed and open-ended architecture can evolve along with critical technologies, providing fixed point of stability for a radiating and long-lived product family. They pointed out clearly that good architectural design of products is not enough, manufacturing decisions are playing an increasing important role in product strategy. Since successful architectures have a high software content, manufacturing skills by themselves are not sufficient.

The authors presented also their belief that architectural competition is stimulating the development of a new form of business organization. They called this new structure the Silicon Valley Model. This was because of the fact that early companies competing with architectures had noticed that they faced the same problems in managing organizations that they faced with technologies and architectures. As an organizational paradigm, the Silicon Valley Model has the following characteristics. Organizational structure and decision making should mirror the technical architecture of the company, technical expertise is required for a large fraction of senior management, and communication should occur directly between relevant parties. Companies need also tight internal proprietary control of architecture while externalizing commodities and niches.

Recently, the role of product architecture has emerged as an important factor not only in the case of IT companies but rather in the case of all companies producing technical products and services. Baldwin and Clark (1997) noticed that increasing technical complexity of many products has forced companies to share the large product projects among several partners. Therefore, companies have to design modular architectures where interfaces between individual parts are well defined. Standardization of these interfaces makes smaller companies competitive. The complexity of the product increases motivation to use subcontractors in the product development and production process.

B.   Product architecture and core competencies

Henderson (1991) related the fragmentary innovative human knowledge and product architectures of a firm. She called "architectural knowledge" the important innovative insights and wisdom required to integrate the diverse bodies of component knowledge. This knowledge is tacit and it is imbedded in the organization, communication channels, information filters, and product solving strategies of experienced product designers. A product design effort will produce both a product and the knowledge created in design teams. Henderson argued that radical innovation, where not only some modules but the product structure and linkages change, may cause great difficulties for the companies because the existing organizational linkages and knowledge channels may be destroyed. Therefore, they proposed that companies should manage their architectural knowledge as a strategic weapon. To help companies to manage architectural knowledge explicitly Henderson classified innovation into four different categories based on the change of linkages and change of core concepts (modules). If both change then the innovation is radical, if only core concepts are reinforced then the innovation is incremental and less risky.

Meyer and Utterbach (1993) pointed out that the product family generated from the common core architecture can be used as a basis for assessing the dynamics of a firm's core capabilities, in other words, how these capabilities grow, decline, and integrate with each other over extent periods of time. They used product family to name the set of products that share a common platform but have specific features and functionality required by different customers. Their article demonstrated how the concept of product family could benefit business managers in analyzing the evolution of their product architecture and identifying the core capabilities of their organizations.

C.   Product platform

The concept of product platform emerged gradually in the context of engineering design and product development in late 1980's. The concept of platform is in relation to so called "platform products" and "technology-push" products. In their development, the origin of the product design was not the traditional specification of customer needs but a technology innovation, adapted later to real market needs. The main idea of product platform was to offer a flexible enabling common base (core of the design architecture) that could generate derivative products easily from the same core. One of the pioneering works in the above area was Wheelwright and Clark's book (1992) with some of the early ideas. Meyer and Utterbach (1993) argument that the vital issue in product development is concentration at the level of the product family, and more specifically on the development of and sharing of key components and assets. The benefit is that firms will then develop the foundation for a range of individual product variations. At an even broader level, one can examine relationships between product families themselves to achieve even greater communality in both technologies and marketing. In their conclusions they offered a more broad definition for the product family such that it should include common product platform, common user needs, common distribution channels, and common manufacturing technologies.

Meyer and Lopez (1995) defined a product platform as the core technologies that are common to all members of a product family. They used the expression of "a platform design" to mean the subsystems or modules and the interfaces between these modules. For an effective design, the interfaces should be seamless and standardized. They showed in their article that the concept of product platform could be productively used to study and improve management of streams of closely related products derived from a common technology platform. They argued for a technology strategy inclusive of all necessary technologies required in current and future product architectures. In addition, they proposed a product family map to understand the evolution of technology strategy and its relationship to the architecture of products and firm performance.

Meyer and Zack (1996) applied the concept of product platform created for physical products quite directly as such into information products. The products used in their examples were different versions of a common data base content, coded on several different media and including a variety of user interfaces. They argued that companies producing information in printed or electronic form can benefit from research on physical products. They argued that information technology companies should address the question of basic and deepest chunks of underlying information units across all the products, and which ones are common and which are specific to particular product offerings. On the basis of this, companies should define what level of granularity of these units can reasonably facilitate a strategy of flexibly mixing and matching different elements together into rapidly created and more fine-tuned customized products.

D.   Product platform strategy

McGrath (1995) introduced the concept of "product platform strategy" in his book on product strategies for high-technology companies. He argued that in order to be successful - perhaps even to survive - a high-technology company must master product strategy. In his four level model the product platform strategies were positioned directly under the strategic vision to give guidelines for the product line strategies and on the individual products.

McGrath pointed out that a product platform is not a product. It is a collection of common elements, specially the underlying core technology, implemented across a range of products. According to McGrath "a platform is in general the lowest level of relevant common technology within the set of products or a product line". The key to a high-technology product platform is the defining (underlying) technology. It establishes the performance characteristics of products based on a platform, provides their basis for differentiation, establishes the limits of their capabilities, and defines their relative costs. Investments in new platforms cannot be justified on the planned success of a single product, but rather need to be evaluated on the expected success of all the resulting products that will be based on that platform. Generation of product platform strategies will help senior management on the most important decisions, establish the foundation for the resulting product line, provides the framework for long-range business strategy, and provides specific direction for technology development.

4. IT infrastructure as platform

The concepts of product platform and IT infrastructure are related in an interesting way. The purpose of building IT infrastructure is to support commonality between different applications or uses. The purpose of product platform is to offer a common core from which a variety of services can be generated to satisfy customer needs.

Both platform and IT infrastructure are technical artifacts that are effective only if they generate useful capabilities. Both are of strategic importance and difficult to imitate, because they integrate and maintain human knowledge and competence. Because of these similarities the idea of platform could be applied in strategic management of IT, specially formulating strategic and implementation plans of corporate IT infrastructure to make it more effective. "IT infrastructure platform" is the common base (core) from which business applications and services will be generated, either as standard services or as their customized derivatives.

The above platform approach to IT infrastructure means a radically different strategic alignment instead of the traditional way. IT strategy and IT infrastructure will be the main drivers to support business applications, not business strategy. We argue that this approach could improve responsiveness of IT infrastructure as the base of future business applications and services, and it may help senior management in their decisions concerning IT infrastructure.

Among the benefits from applying product platform strategy to develop corporate IT infrastructure are the following:
- Senior management will understand the purpose of IT infrastructure as a whole
- IT infrastructure decisions will be more concrete, focusing on the core of corporate information systems architecture and underlying technology

- IT infrastructure based "service level" alignment will be more effective than "business strategy execution" based, specially if the business marketplace is highly volatile
- Substantial benefits come from better responsiveness, flexibility, customization of services, and cost effectiveness of the infrastructure.

One extra benefit from formulation infrastructure strategy as a platform strategy is better coordination of outsourcing relations with IT vendors. Integration of external software product platforms of potential vendors into the corporate IT infrastructure is easier.

Applying platform strategy into development of corporate IT infrastructure would in practice mean the following major change of the typical working procedure. Frequent corporate-wide surveys of possible changes of future business strategies and needs as well as difficult speculations of possible reconstruction of the existing infrastructure will not be the primary problems. Major IT infrastructure decisions focus carefully on the enabling common core of the IT infrastructure platform. Only this common core will be implemented and it will be reused in the future infrastructure extensions, when the very real business needs are exactly known. Only at some point of time in the future, more extensive redesign of the IT infrastructure is needed.

5.   Summary and conclusions

Our literature review showed that the concept of product platform was originally almost identical with an implemented and reusable core of the product architecture, based on common technology and having the purpose to generate a whole product family. Broadly speaking, the concept has expanded to contain understanding of customer needs, marketing channels, service mechanisms, and even manufacturing processes. Sometimes, the product platform architecture is a dominant driver of the organizational structure of the firm (the Silicon Valley Model). A product platform may maintain valuable core competence that can be destroyed if the product architecture, specially the linkages, undergoes a radical change. Relevant product platform strategies may help senior management greatly in decisions concerning product development and core competency, and make the product development more effective.

IT infrastructure is the enabling base of the shared IT capabilities that provide the foundation for other business systems. Also, IT infrastructure is in relation to technology architecture, the architecture of corporate information systems. In product platform terms, IT infrastructure is the common core of future business applications and services, from which the actual applications and services are derived.

We proposed application of the product platform idea to help in strategic decision making concerning the corporate IT infrastructure. Then, instead of planning for a fixed and complete IT infrastructure based on the commonality of various future business needs, the strategic decision should be limited to the common core of the future IT infrastructure, together with definition of under-lying technology. We argued that this IT infrastructure platform based approach has considerable benefits, specially in the case of a highly volatile business marketplace and in the case of virtual organization.

On the basis of the arguments presented, we propose that researchers continue conceptual work in order to design prototypal models of IT infrastructure platforms. Also, empirical research is needed to study how different IT infra-structure platforms may differ and how these differences are related to key business attributes of the company.

Markku SAAKSJARVI

Résumé

Les concepts de plateforme de produits et d'infrastructure informationnelle comme outils de management stratégique des technologies de l'information

Ce chapitre présente les nouvelles évolutions en matière de technologies de l'information et de la communication, et leur impact sur la gestion stratégique des entreprises industrielles et de services, et par delà sur leur compétitivité dans un contexte mondial "globalisé".

La mise en oeuvre des technologies informationnelles modernes a considérablement modifié les données de la gestion des entreprises, en faisant émerger de nouveaux *concepts* analytiques tels "infrastructure informationnelle", "plateforme de produits", "architectures technologiques", "réseaux de compétences", "organisations virtuelles". Ces concepts rendent compte d'une *réalité* émergente. Ce sont dès lors de nouveaux types de choix décisionnels qui se dégagent et qui s'inscrivent dans des contraintes de gestion de plus en plus complexes. De nouvelles logiques de développement des firmes apparaissent, basées sur les infrastructures technologiques des systèmes d'information et sur les compétences humaines (savoirs individuels et collectifs) susceptibles de maîtriser, de faire évoluer et de contrôler ces systèmes. Ce sont là de nouvelles barrières à l'entrée et de nouveaux avantages concurrentiels (difficiles à imiter rapidement) qui voient le jour, remettant en cause les anciens modèles de gestion stratégique.

Zusammenfassung

Wirkung der Produktplattform und IT* Infrastruktur auf das Strategische Management

In diesem Beitrag werden die neueren Entwicklungen im Bereich der Informations- und Kommunkationstechnologien dargelegt sowie ihr Einfluß auf das Strategische Management und darüber hinaus auf die Wettbewerbsfähigkeit im globalisierten Kontext der Unternehmen.

Der Einsatz moderner Informationstechnologien hat die Unternehmensführung grundlegend geändert. Neue analytische Konzepte kamen auf wie "Informationsinfrastruktur", "Produktplattform", "technologische Architektur", "Kompetenzvernetzung" "virtuelle Organisation". Das Aufkommen dieser Begriffe steht für das Aufkommen einer neuen Wirklichkeit. In Folge entstehen auch neuartige, immer stärkeren Zwängen unterliegende Entscheidungsabläufe. Neue Entwicklungslogiken werden sichtbar, die auf den Infrastrukturen neuer Informationssysteme und auf individueller wie auch kollektiver Kompetenz der Mitarbeiter beruhen, mit deren Hilfe diese neuen Systeme beherrscht, weiterentwickelt und kontrolliert werden. Neue Zugangsbarrieren und auch neue Wettbewerbsvorteile, die nicht so leicht imitiert werden können, sind so im Entstehen, und die bisherigen Strategiemodelle werden so in Frage gestellt.

---

*   IT = Informations Technologie

References

ALEXANDER, C. (1997): *Notes on the Synthesis of Form*. First printing 1964. Harvard University Press. Boston MA.

BALDWIN, C./CLARK, K. (1997): Managing in the Age of Modularity. *Harvard Business Review*. September-October. 84-93.

BRADLEY, S.P./HAUSMAN, J.A./NOLAN, R.L. (1993): Globalization and Technology. in: Bradley, S.P./Hausman, J.A./Nolan, R.L.: *Globalization, Technology and Competition, The Fusion of Computers and Telecommunications in the 1990s*. Harvard Business School Press. Boston MA.

BROADBENT, M./WEILL, P./O'BRIEN, T./NEO, B.S. (1996): Firm Context and Patterns of IT Infrastructure Capability. in: DeGross, J.I./Jarvenpaa, S./ Srinivasan, A. (Editors): *Proceedings of the Seventeenth International Conference on Information Systems*. 174-194.

BROADBENT, M./WEILL, P. (1997): Management by Maxim: How Business and IT Managers Can Create IT Infrastructures. *Sloan Management Review*. Spring. 77-92.

DAVIDOW, W.H./MALONE, M.S. (1992): *The Virtual Corporation*. Harper Collins. New York.

HENDERSON, R. (1991): Architectural Innovation as a Source of Competitive Advantage. *Design Management Journal*. N° 2. Summer. 43-47.

HENDERSON, J.C./VENKATRAMAN, N. (1993): Strategic Alignment: Leveraging Information Technology for Transforming Organizations. *IBM Systems Journal*. Vol 32. N° 1. 4-16.

IS ANALYZER (1991): Building Global IT Infrastructure. *IS Analyzer*. June 29. 1-16.

McGRATH, M.E. (1995): *Product Strategy for High-Technology Companies*. Richard D. Irvin. Homewood Ill.

MEYER, M.H./LOPEZ, L. (1995): Technology Strategy in a Products Company. *Journal of Product Innovation Management*, 12. 294-306.

MEYER, M.H./TERZAKIAN, P./UTTERBACH, J.M. (1997): Metrics for Managing Research and Development in the Context of the Product Family. *Management Science*. Vol. 43. N° 1. January. 88-111.

MEYER, M.H./UTTERBACH, J.M. (1993): The Product Family and the Dynamics of Core Capability. *Sloan Management Review*. Spring. 29-47.

MEYER, M.H./ZACK, M.H (1996): The Design and Development of Information products. *Sloan management Review*. Spring. 43-59.

MILLER, D.B./CLEMONS, E.K./ROW, M.C. (1993): Information Technology and the Global Virtual Corporation. in: Bradley, S.P./Hausman, J.A./Nolan, R.L. (Editors): *Globalization, Technology and Competition, The Fusion of Computers and Telecommunications in the 1990s*. Harvard Business School Press. Boston MA.

MORRIS, C.R./FERGUSON, C.H. (1993): How Architecture Wins Technology Wars. *Harvard Business Review*. March-April. 86-96.

PINE II, J. (1993): *Mass Customization: The Next Frontier of Business Competition*. Harvard School Press. Boston MA.

SOWA, J.F./ZACHMAN, J.A. (1992): Extending and Formalizing the Framework for Information Systems Architecture. *IBM Systems Journal, 31* (3).

WHEELWRIGHT, S.C./CLARK, K.B. (1992): Revolutionizing New product Development. Free Press. New-York.

ZACHMAN, J.A. (1987): A Framework for Information Systems Architecture. *IBM Systems Journal, 26* (3).

Yves De Rongé

The Impact of New Information and Communication Technologies on Management Control Systems

1. Introduction

2. Information technology and organizational change

3. The classical characteristics of a management control system
    A. Consistency with the organizational structure
    B. Coherence with the chosen strategy

4. Information technology and management control systems in the functional organization
    A. Characteristics of the functional organization
    B. The main characteristics of management control systems in a functional hierarchical organization
    C. The role of information technology in the functional organization

5. Information technology and management control systems in the firm of the 90's
    A. The growing crisis of the functional view of the organization
    B. The characteristics of a process view of the organization
    C. The development of management control systems adapted to a process view of the organization
    D. The role of new information and communication technologies on the management control of process organizations

6. Conclusion

---

1. Introduction

The aim of this chapter is to look at the development of new information and communication technologies and to assess their relevance for organizations that need to change their strategy and structure, and consequently their management control systems (MCS), to adapt to a more challenging environment, characterized by constant change.

We show that the first introduction of information technology in organizations allowed the automation of the organization according to their functional lines while more recent information and communication technologies are well suited to sustain a process view of the organization.

The rest of the chapter is organized as follows. The first section presents a short summary of the main theories examining the impact of information technology on organizational change. The second section briefly summarizes the main characteristics of classical management control systems. The third section deals with the functional organization. After a brief reminder of the main characteristics of a functional organization, its management control systems are briefly discussed. The section ends with a discussion of the impact of information technology on MCS. The last section looks at more recent organizational structures based on the activity and process concepts. The developments of MCS for process organizations are briefly discussed. The final part is devoted to the impact of new information and communication technologies such as integrated software, groupware, intranets and data warehouses on management control systems.

2. Information technology and organizational change

In this section, our ambition is not to present a thorough literature review of the impact of the development of information and communication technologies on organizations and in particular on control and decision making in organizations but to select some of the theoretical points, relevant for our purposes, that have been elaborated regarding this question, looking at various fields, such as management control literature, information technology literature and organizational change literature.

Markus and Robey (1988) present an interesting paper looking at various theories trying to explain the links between information technology and organizational change. They distinguish three main theoretical approaches regarding the causal agent in the relationship between IT and organizational change[1]:

1. the *technological imperative* that "views technology as an exogenous force which determines or strongly constrains the behavior of individuals or organizations"[2]. According to this perspective, the increasing use of IT would lead to an increased centralization in the organizations. Empirical evidence does not support this contention. Robey (1977) found that IT supports a decentralized structure when there is a large uncertainty and supports a centralized structure when the environment is more stable. Malone (1997) shows that first IT developments have led to increased centralization when communication costs decrease, and that most recent information and communication technology developments that allow a further decrease in communication costs seem to lead to increased decentralization, giving birth to organizations composed of connected, decentralized decision makers;

2. the *organizational imperative* considers that managers are designing the information systems in order to satisfy the informational needs of the organization. As an example of such an approach, Macintosh (1985) develops a contextual or contingent model of accounting and information systems. He uses the definition of technology, in terms of task variety and task knowledge, proposed by Perrow (1967) that leads to four major types of technology: routine, craft, technical-professional and research. He proposes then four types of management control systems that are related to these technology types:

---

[1]   A similar characterization is proposed by R. Reix (1990).
[2]   Markus and Robey, 1988, p. 585.

- a close management control system adapted to routine technology characterized by very frequent reporting of specific, detailed data, defined by the top management;
- a results oriented MCS for craft technology with infrequent reporting of general data;
- a comprehensive MCS for a technical-professional technology with less frequent reporting than for the routine technology, with specific and detailed statistical reports and very general budget information;
- a prospects-oriented MCS for a research technology with little detail, infrequent reporting and a bottom-up approach.

3. the *emergent perspective* that claims that the "uses and consequences of information technology emerge unpredictably from complex social interactions"[3]. The technology creates the opportunity for an organizational change but, before implementing it, it is impossible to predict which change will emerge from the large choice of alternatives that exist. According to this view, it is possible to predict that something will emerge but not to predict what exactly will emerge of the complex social interactions that occur when a new information technology is introduced. A large amount of recent empirical evidence seems to confirm that perspective.

This last perspective will be retained in this contribution when looking at the impact of information and communication technologies on management control systems.

3.   The classical characteristics of a management control system

We use here the traditional definition of R. Anthony (1988) who defines three levels of control in an organization: strategic planning, management control and task control. Strategic planning is defined as "the process of deciding on the goals of the organization and the strategies for attaining these goals"[4].

---

[3]   Markus and Robey, op. cit., p. 588.
[4]   Anthony R. (1988), p. 10.

Management control is "the process by which managers influence other members of the organization to implement the organization's strategies"[5]. Task control is "the process of assuring that specified tasks are carried out effectively and efficiently"[6]. Such a definition of what is management control attributes an essential role to the accounting information in the control process.

Based on the distinctions made by H. Simon (1960) between programmed and non-programmed decisions, Gorry and Scott-Morton (1971, 1989) have shown that the three levels of control as defined by Anthony were relative to different types of decision making. The operational (task) control level was made of structured, programmed decisions. The management control consists of semi-structured decisions while the strategic planning is made of unstructured, non-programmed decisions. The different nature of the managerial activities conducted at these various levels lead to different need in terms of management information systems.

These three levels of control are clearly interdependent and the coherence of their interrelations is an important factor in the contribution of management control systems to a company's competitiveness. Keeping in mind the relationships between the different levels of the control system, our analysis will focus on the level of management control as defined supra[7].

Under the classical paradigm developed by Anthony, the main instruments of the management control system are the programming, the budgeting process,

---

[5]   ibidem, p. 10.

[6]   ibidem, p. 12.

[7]   This vision of management control that constitutes the main paradigm has been submitted to fundamental criticisms by some authors. A critical assessment of this paradigm has been developed among others by T. Lowe and T. Puxty (1989). They stress the narrowness of such a definition that does not take into account the environment in which the organization is located, the multiple interrelations between the three control levels and that it limits the control to a simple feedback process.

the transfer pricing system, the performance evaluation and the incentive and compensation plans[8].

The objective of controlling the implementation of strategies by the members of the organization assigned to management control has two main consequences regarding its structure:
1. the consistency with the organizational structure;
2. the coherence with the strategy chosen by the organizational unit.

A.   Consistency with the organizational structure

Each company has chosen an organizational structure, either functional, multi-divisional or matrix, to do business. It is not unusual that the growth of a company leads the top management to change the organizational structure through time in order to better adapt the organization to the environment where it is located and to the characteristics of the businesses it has chosen. It is of great importance to build a management control system well fitted to the specificities of the organizational structure chosen by top management. Programming, the role and implementation of a budgeting process are completely different in a functional organization or in a multidivisional company with many unrelated businesses. In a multidivisional company, the type of information relevant for decision making is not the same for the corporate management and for the divisional managements and the management control systems implemented must take into account this diversity of informational needs. Different management control systems could coexist in the same company depending on the organizational structure and the different strategic orientations chosen by each of the businesses that constitute the company.

---

[8]   Such a list of control instruments shows clearly the main place taken by the accounting system in the control process.

B.   Coherence with the chosen strategy

Different strategies require different management control systems. Each control system, based on performance measures, has an impact on the behavior of the members of the organization whose performance is evaluated[9]. It is therefore important that management control systems lead to a behavior compatible with the strategy chosen by the top management.

Four main strategies are generally advised depending on the position of a product or a business in its life cycle:
1. a "build" strategy advised when a company launches a new product;
2. a "hold" strategy that aims at maintaining and developing the market share and the competitive position of a product in the growth phase;
3. a "harvest" strategy whose goal is to maximize revenues and short terms cash flows during the maturity phase;
4. a "divest" strategy at the end of the maturity phase.

M. Porter (1980) proposes two different strategies that enable a company to build a sustainable competitive advantage: cost leadership or differentiation.

A performing management control system must be designed in such a way that the members of the organization have a behavior compatible with the strategic objectives chosen by the company.

3.   Information technology and management control systems in the functional organization

After a brief characterization of the organizational principles underlying the functional organization, the basic management control systems characteristic of this model are presented and the role of information technology in this framework is discussed.

---

[9]   In this sense, management control is more similar to a control of the individuals in the organization than a control of the organization as such.

A.   Characteristics of the functional organization

Management control systems have been first developed to help decision making and control in a functional organization devised according the principles of the scientific management school led by Taylor and Fayol, for instance. The Taylorian vision of the organization is grounded on a set of assumptions that translate relatively well the economic world at the beginning of this century:
- an assumption of stability of the economic environment, and in particular of the technology, the competition and the critical success factors of performance;
- an assumption that top management possesses perfect information regarding the economy, the competition and the technological evolution on one side and regarding the main economic determinants of successful economic performance on the other side;
- an assumption that organizations are simple and may be perfectly modelled from the top, even by an outsider. Their functioning may be represented by a set of standardized programmed processes.

On the basis of these assumptions, the main characteristics of the functional organization have been constructed. They are summarized hereafter:
- organizations may be decomposed into organizational units where similar activities will be conducted. The principle of division of labor leads to an increased specialization of each of these organizational units where similar competencies have been grouped. Each organizational unit defines, according to its competence's logic, an optimal way of conducting the activities in which they are specialized;
- the optimal performance of the organization as a whole is obtained by summing up the optimal local performances of the various organizational units that constitute the company;
- the organization's performance depends essentially on the optimization of the internal functioning of the organization. In an economy dominated by producers where demand is greater then supply, it is not necessary to manage value and company profits are essentially driven by cost control inside the organization;

- the production cost is highly correlated with one main production factor, labor. Controlling labor costs will assure the company's global performance.

The organization is seen as a set of independent functions regrouping similar competences that are optimized locally according to their specialized competences. Communication between functions is unusual and occurs only between the various functional top managers. The coordination is achieved at the top of the organization. Interdependencies between functions are weak and are managed and coordinated by the hierarchy.

This Taylorian view of the organization leads to a management control based on the hierarchy. Management control systems were organized in order to provide adequate information for decision making and control along the hierarchical lines. This type of organization is based on a top down approach of command and control.

B. The main characteristics of management control systems in a functional hierarchical organization

In the functional organization, hierarchy is the dominant control mode. Long term objectives have been defined by top management and are translated into annual plans by the management control department, a staff function at the corporate level. Annual budgets play a crucial role in the functional organization because it is the main coordination and communication tool between functions that work independently. Goal congruence between various functions optimizing locally according to their own set of specialized competences, is in effect obtained by budgets. Budgets assign authority on a specified set of resources being human, material or technical to organizational units and define objectives that have to be reached by them. Once their budget is established, each organizational unit makes management decisions in order to reach the local objective that it has been assigned. The performance of the company as a whole is obtained by the local achievement of the budgeted objectives.

The other components of the management control systems are essentially driven by budgets. Performance evaluation systems track the use of resources assigned to the organizational units and compare at prespecified periods the actual results attained by the unit with the objectives assigned. Incentive and reward systems are based essentially on the achievement of budget objectives.

The management control systems described are perfectly coherent with the assumptions underlying the Taylorian principles of organization, i.e. stability of the environment that is a necessary condition to use budget as a planning and control tool and an assumption of perfect information of the top management that allows them to define in advance a set of objectives by function that will allow the company to reach its long term objectives.

C.   The role of information technology in the functional organization

Information technology was first introduced in the fifties to automate existing routine tasks. The focus was on reducing the costs of processing a number of standard routinized transactions in the organization. Information technology was essentially used to automate the existing business processes in the organization. The mainframe computer systems introduced in large companies in the beginning of the sixties were built according to a systems architecture that embedded a centralized control of information processing. As shown by R. Nolan and D. Croson (1995) this computer architecture was in harmony with the control principles of the hierarchy in functional organizations. Information systems were designed in such a way that they replicate the existing business practices and were consequently designed according to functional lines. Manufacturing informations systems deal with manufacturing operations, marketing informations systems are constructed to help decision making in marketing. These various information systems are designed independently by each function and the transfer of marketing information to the manufacturing people is relatively difficult because the informations systems have not been built in order to facilitate or allow cross functional sharing of information.

In functional organizations, information technology developments were gradually introduced with the purpose of speeding up existing business processes and reducing the amount of resources consumed by the performing of business transactions.

In summary, information technology was essentially used to automate existing processes and to decrease the cost of operating them. This was coherent with the underlying Taylorian vision of the organization according to which perfect information on the organization and the environment combined with the stability of competitive and technological environments to permit the identification of the "one best way" to manage any business process. The information technology was used to reduce the cost of operating the "one best way".

Since the seventies, major developments in the economy and technology have lead to a growing questioning of the relevance and adequacy of the functional organization for actual business challenges.

4. Information technology and management control systems in the firm of the 90's

After a short analysis of the growing crisis of the traditional functional organization, the main characteristics of an emerging form of cross-functional, transversal organization are discussed and the contribution of new information and communication technologies to their management control systems is assessed.

A. The growing crisis of the functional view of the organization

The economic environment in which many companies have been operating for twenty years has been subject to massive changes that can be summarized in three main evolutions:
- increased competition that is becoming global in a world moving from standardized mass production to customized production where the determi-

nants of economic performance are now multiple and depend as much on quality, time and innovation as on cost;
- increased deregulation of large industrial and service sectors that are no longer protected from competition;
- increased rhythm of technological innovation that leads to a decrease in product life cycles and a blurring of the boundaries between industries and technologies as for example in the computer, image and telecommunication industries.

These major changes in the economic environment have led to the need for alternative forms of organizational structure that take into account the cross-functional dimension of the business.

J. Child (1987) has remarkably analyzed the role information technology can play in meeting the strategic challenges created by the new environment and helping to sustain the new organizational arrangements needed to operate in these new business conditions. The three main strategic challenges that he identifies are the following:
- to cope with the demand risk caused by sharp fluctuations in demand for products and services;
- to manage the innovation risk, caused by the increased pace of technological change that a company needs to adapt to constantly;
- to control the inefficiency risk, caused by the increased competition based on cost control and reduction.

Companies need to adopt alternative organizational forms than the Taylorian functional form to deal with these main strategic challenges. Child identifies six different modes of organizing transactions and illustrates the role IT can play in their management.

In this paper, we will focus on a vision of the organization as a set of activities and processes as an alternative to the traditional functional firm and illustrate the role that NICT[10] can play in the management control of organizations focused on their main processes.

B.   The characteristics of a process view of the organization

An organization can be seen as a set of processes that regroup a set of activities. These two concepts are briefly defined in the next paragraphs.

- The concept of activity

The most current definition of activity used in accounting and management control literature states that an activity is a set of related tasks conducted by an entity of the organization. The activity of supplier certification entails a set of related tasks that lead to an output: a supplier being certified. The undertaking of the activity needs the combination of several inputs (labor, raw material, technology, methods, information,...) to obtain an output, product or service, for a customer being internal, i.e. inside the firm, or external, i.e. the final customer[11]. This concept is not limited to the production function but is easily applicable to all functions of the organization (R&D, marketing, human resources, MIS,...).

The organization seen as a set of activities is defined on the basis of what is done in the company and no longer on the basis of a grouping of specialized competences in specific functions.

The value of an activity is measured by its contribution to the final customer's satisfaction. Managing customer value can be made by managing activities from the point of view of their value for the final customer.

---

10   for New Information and Communication Technologies.

11   It should be noted however that there is a fundamental difference between an internal and an external customer to an activity or a process : the external customer values the product or service of the firm by deciding to buy it. His satisfaction determines the long term profitability and therefore survival of the firm.

- The concept of process

A process is constituted by a set of activities that often belong to different functions and are thus transversal to the functional organization. A process is a set of interrelated activities undertaken to obtain a global output for a customer, being internal or external. Lorino (1996) defines the process as "a set of activities linked with each other by significant information flows that combine with each other to provide an important and well defined tangible or intangible product"[12]. Hammer and Champy (1993) define the business process as "a collection of activities that takes one or more kinds of input and creates an output that is of value to the customer"[13].

A major characteristic of the processes is that they are cross functional by linking together different activities that are undertaken in organizational units that belong to different functions.

The concepts of activity and process introduce an alternative to the Taylorian functional view of the organization. The process view of the organization advocates a global optimization that aims at reducing the total cost of the process by optimizing the linkages between the various activities that constitute the process, instead of focusing attention and efforts on the local optimization of each activity, part of a process[14].

An example may help to grasp the main differences between the functional view and the process view of the organization. The purchasing function is managed differently in a functional firm than in a process-oriented firm.

In the functional firm, the purchasing department often receives an objective of negotiating lower prices with suppliers for a desired level of quality. By focusing

---

[12] See Lorino P.(1996), p. 55. Translation by the author.
[13] See Hammer M. and Champy (1993), p. 35.
[14] This view of the organization as a set of processes is close to the value chain concept of the organization proposed by Porter (1985).

94

on its departmental objectives of purchasing cost minimization, the department will adopt a purchasing policy that has the following characteristics:
- deal with a large number of suppliers and select the ones that offer the lower prices;
- often buy in large quantities in order to obtain large discounts.

This purchasing policy may be underoptimal for the company as a whole because it creates additional costs for the other departments of the organization (high defect rates because of the slightly lower quality of raw materials, large storage facilities, high complexity and cost of inventory management,...).

The process view of the organization looks at the inbound logistics process. The whole set of activities being part of the process needs to be identified: selection and certification of suppliers, purchase orders creation, order administration, orders payment, quality control of deliveries, storage, material handling to the production floor... The process view leads to a completely different definition of a purchasing policy: selection of a small number of suppliers with the same set of characteristics (financial strength, ISO 9000 certification, JIT suppliers,...) with whom the firm can enter into long term partnerships. This policy leads to a cost minimization of the purchasing policy for the firm as a whole.

C. The development of management control systems adapted to a process view of the organization

In a rapidly changing environment and with the adoption of a process view of the organization, management control systems need to be redefined in order to help manage continuous change instead of a relative stability in business conditions. In this part, we will briefly discuss two main developments of management control systems that are particularly relevant for a process view of the organization: the ABC/ABM model and the Simons model that identifies four different levers of control.

- The ABC/ABM model

The structuring of a company according to its activities shows what the company does and how it does it. The activities map generally differs from the company's organizational chart that is structured according to the responsibilities granted to the members of the organization. The division by activities, by emphasizing the interdependences between activities beyond their functional membership, generally does not correspond to the responsibilities defined by the organizational chart.

Activity Based Management leads to a different perspective in terms of management control systems. Their role is not so much to allocate resources between the different functions in the company and to put in place a system to control the effective and efficient use of the allocated resources but to focus on the continuous improvement of processes by promoting organizational learning and innovation. ABM allows at the same time:
- a diagnostic role, identifying the constitutive drivers of performance and their relationships[15];
- and a steering role, allowing the implementation of the strategy in the most effective way.

- The Simons model of management control: the four levers of control

Simons (1994) has studied in depth the way companies use their management control systems to effectively implement their strategies. He defines management control systems as being "the formal, information-based routines and procedures managers use to maintain or alter patterns in organizational activities"[16].

---

[15] Activity Based Costing is an accounting information system that sustain the implementation of the Activity Based Management. The activity replaces the functional department as cost pool where indirect costs to the cost object measured are traced.
[16] Simons R., 1994, p. 5.

For Simons (1995), the main problem faced by management control systems in today's companies, illustrated by recent major control failures such as in the Barings case and other respectable companies that have occurred large losses because of control failures, is the balance between creating the necessary empowerment to allow enough flexibility to adapt to ever changing customer tastes, technology and competition and ensuring a sufficient control of empowered managers. This balance may be obtained by simultaneously using four different levers of control:

– diagnostic control systems similar to those used in Taylorian organizations. They function on the feedback mode of control. Critical performance variables are checked regularly and compared with expected standards of performance. Deviations from standards trigger actions by management to bring the process back in control;

– beliefs systems have the purpose of creating a set of core values that are shared by all the organization's members. Empowered individuals look for opportunities in the environment and for new initiatives that are coherent with the values and the purpose of the organization they belong to;

– boundary systems state the rules of the game, establish a set of actions or behaviors that are forbidden by the company (bribery, violation of legal rules,...) and define the limits one should not trespass. These boundary systems are often embedded in codes of ethical conduct;

– interactive control systems are "the formal information systems that managers use to involve themselves regularly and personally in the decisions of subordinates"[17]. These systems are used by senior managers to "focus organizational attention and learning on key strategic issues"[18]. According to Simons[19], they have four major characteristics:

  • they track information that has been identified as potentially strategic by top management and that is often changing;
  • this information is significant enough to request regular and frequent attention from operational managers;

---

[17]   Simons R., 1995, p. 86.
[18]   Simons R., op. cit., p. 86.
[19]   ibidem, p. 87.

- the meaningful interpretation of the information generated by the inter-active control systems necessitates regular face-to-face meetings between superiors, subordinates and peers;
- the system leads to an ongoing exchange concerning data, assumptions and action plans.

These new management control systems are heavily dependent on the new information and communication technologies that are presented and discussed in the next part.

D.   The role of new information and communication technologies in the management control of process organizations

Recent developments in information and communication technologies have greatly enhanced the possibility of developing management control systems well adapted to the informational needs of the process organization. As has already been mentioned, previous automation led to the development of functional MIS which were independently developed and poorly interconnected. Moving from a functional view to a process view of the organization is only possible if MIS can be developed that allow cross functional sharing of information. Several developments in information and communications technologies have made that possible. Among others, we have selected four new developments in information and communication technology:
- integrated softwares;
- groupware technologies;
- Internet and intranets;
- data warehousing.

- Integrated software

The most successful integrated software for business process management is proposed by a German company SAP whose two main products-R/2 devised for mainframes and R/3 designed for client-server architectures are adopted by a growing number of companies. The SAP System is a large set of software applications in real time that covers all major business functions such as Materials Management, Production Planning and Control, Costing, Maintenance, Financial Accounting, Assets Management, Cost Accounting, Project Management, Sales Management, Invoicing, Shipping and Human Resources Management.

The SAP system has a modular structure and a company can choose to implement only part of the modules proposed in the integrated SAP system. The different modules corresponding to the various business functions are articulated around a teleprocessing and database management system (DB/DC system).

In a well functioning MIS, information is entered once in the system and is available and stable for the various functions that may need the same information. This SAP solution combines centralized data processing with decentralized data entering and access. The various implementations of SAP I have observed in three very different types of organizations (large oil company, medium wireworks company and an university), illustrate the emergent perspective on the effect of IT on organizational change. Business process redesign is often undertaken after the decision to implement SAP has been made and the software is not implemented to sustain a new organizational design but leads to changes in the business processes while the software is implemented.

From a management control perspective, SAP implementation in the large oil company leads to a clear improvement of the control properties of the MIS for corporate management when it replaces decentralized MIS by countries and by functions[20]. For example, the corporate management of that company has access much more quickly to well defined and standardized accounting information that allows the corporate assessment and comparison (benchmarking) of the relative performances of each subsidiary. A common language has been created throughout the organization.

---

[20]   For a detailed analysis, see De Rongé Y. and Cerrada K. (1996).

The question that appears here is whether such an integrated management information system is able to replace the local MIS to generate the relevant financial, production and sales information for decision making in the various marketing subsidiaries. It enhanced centralized management control but is not necessarily perfectly adapted to the informational needs of local decision makers in the various subsidiaries.

The retail industry has also seen dramatic changes in operations following the introduction of integrated software combined with new communication technologies. A recent paper by J. Frances and E. Garnsey illustrates how information and telecommunication technologies have been used by supermarkets to redesign their relationships with their suppliers. These innovations have considerably lowered the costs of the processes linking the suppliers to the supermarkets.

The development of integrated software has allowed better communication and better coordination between functions and can sustain the business processes of the organization. It allows companies to deal with the inefficiency risk as defined by Child (1987) (cfr supra).

- Groupware technologies

The move from a functional view to a process view of the organization creates new informational needs to assure adequate communication and coordination between the various organization members involved in specific processes that are transversal to the functional organization.

The first definition of groupware states that "Groupware is intentional GROUP processes and procedures to achieve specific purposes plus SoftWARE tools designed to support and facilitate group work"[21].

---

[21]   definition given in 1981 by P&T Johnson-Lentz.

This technology appears particularly well adapted to a process view of the organization. Groupware can be defined as collaboration software in the sense that it helps work groups to accomplish group assignments. It includes software applications for computer conferencing, electronic mail, BBS, project management, file sharing, scheduling meetings and work flow.

Groupware techology is designed to help the work group, defined as two or more people working together on the same assignment. A work group may consist of members belonging to the same functional department and carrying together a common activity. But it may also consist of people belonging to different departments, in different geographical locations and working together for a limited time period on a specific project. In this case, information and communications technologies will allow group members to work together by bypassing time constraints, geographical distances and organizational boundaries.

It has been recently argued that management control should evolve from a pure planning and control function towards a steering function of the organization. People in organizations construct their own interpretation of the activities they are part of and one major role management control systems should play in this regard is to contribute to build a shared vision and interpretation of the processes that constitute the organization. Lorino (1995) advocates the move from a measurement perspective on management control to a more interpretative role for the management control function, in the sense of managing and steering the interpretations of the organization members towards the goals of the organization. Some authors, like Briole, Craipeau and Faguet-Picq (1997) have shown that groupware technologies share the same underlying logic as the activity and process model of the organization. Groupware technologies can bring a major contribution by increasing cohesion in decentralized organizations. It can help the continuous improvement of coordination between activities chained into a process and increase the capacity of organizations to manage interdependencies. Groupware technologies may help to ensure coordination in the organization and may lead to a decrease in the role of hierarchy as the main coordination principle in the functional organization.

Electronic mail is, for instance, a very powerful means of communication that allows members of the organization to communicate across hierarchical boundaries, i.e. allowing people situated at very different positions in the hierarchy to communicate directly, bypassing their immediate superior or subordinate, accelerating information transmission and alleviating the information bias problem.

In conclusion, one can argue that groupware technologies are the enabling information and communication technology which enables the building of management control systems that sustain the process view. By allowing constant communication between physically dispersed organization members, groupware technologies help to maintain and develop the integration of large companies, composed of a large number of decentralized and geographically dispersed organizational units. In this regard, they bring a major contribution to one of the main management control functions: ensure the goal congruence of increasingly decentralized organizational units.

- The development of the Internet and company's intranets

The Internet has been defined as a "network of networks" or as "a loose collection of related computer networks". It has considerably multiplied the communication possibilities open to people and companies at an ever decreasing cost. The development of the Internet and of hypertext language has opened the possibility to communicate and exchange data between computers of different types and various operating systems. The Internet offers numerous possibilities to develop electronic commerce.

As has been mentioned before, the first wave of automation has led to the development of information systems according to functional lines. Different departments had various computer types and different software applications that were inaccessible to each other. The Internet technology has helped companies to solve that problem by building what is now called intranets. They may be defined as user-friendly internal corporate networks using internet technology. Large companies are building intranets that use the infrastructure and services of the Internet but in a private network, inaccessible to outsiders. It is probably today the cheapest and more efficient way of building an information network for a large geographically dispersed global company. Companies are using intranets to sustain various business processes such as the sales cycle for example.

Intranets allow companies to link together isolated islands of information technology investments done in the various departments. They sustain a radical shift in the way information is managed in the company. Information was run on a functional basis and there was no cross-functional communication of the information except at the top of the organization between functional managers. It was not rare that in various parts of the same company, different people were looking after the same information and building databases with the same information. The intranet is based on the reverse assumption that shared information in the company is one of the most valuable assets of a company.

Intranets are also used to manage knowledge in a company. It allows the sharing of knowledge of all the members of the company, as knowledge is becoming the most important intangible asset in a growing number of companies. Management consultants have developed highly efficient intranets to share the valuable knowledge of all their partners in the whole world.

One important role of management control systems is to manage information. Intranets open a radically different way of managing the information that is once again highly compatible with a process view of the organization. Information on all the activities that are part of the same process is now easily available to all functions involved in the process.

* Data warehousing

A corporate data warehouse is defined by Kelly (1996) as a "single integrated store of data which provides the infrastructural basis for informational software applications in the enterprise"[22]. The data warehouse is built in order to support the decision making processes of the organization by putting together all data available in the various departments of the organization and linking these data together with external data that are collected and stored.

A typical data warehouse will combine and integrate in a meaningful way internal data coming from the various previously isolated functional databases existing in the organization and external data coming from different sources. Internal data that will feed the data warehouse comes from the various financial systems (general ledger, cost accounting,...), logistics systems, production systems (MRPII for instance), sales and marketing systems, human resource systems, information systems. External data such as competitor data, customer data, supplier data and economic data must be acquired often by using the services of specialized information providers.

By integrating data of the various functions the data warehouse is a powerful tool to sustain the implementation and control of a process view of the organization. By combining internal and external data, it can also be used as a strategic information system to track changes in demand and tastes of customers, constantly adapting production to the actual tastes and desires of the customers. The retail industry is using data warehouses to identify specific subsets of customers and to design a specific product range for that particular subset. Data warehousing is clearly an important development to deal with demand risk as defined supra.

---

[22]   Kelly S. (1996), p. 55.

6. Conclusion

In the face of an economic and technological environment essentially characterized by constant change, companies need to adapt their organizational strategies and structures in order to be better able to compete in this changing world. Management control systems need also to be redefined in order to be coherent with the strategy and organizational structure necessary in a constantly changing environment.

In this chapter, we have focused on the process organization as one possibility for designing new organizational structures adapted to this new competitive environment. We have shown that there is a high coherence between the new possibilities opened by the development of NICT and the process view of the organization. NICT offer the technical tools to develop management control systems that ensure communication, coordination and goal congruence in the process organization.

More research is necessary to understand what kind of management control systems will emerge with the growing use of NICT in companies organized according to their major processes.

Yves DE RONGE

Résumé

L'impact des nouvelles technologies d'information et de communication sur les systèmes de contrôle des organisations

Les entreprises ont à gérer un changement constant et rapide. Les technologies informationnelles constituent à la fois une cause et un moyen de ce changement qui se répercute en particulier sur les systèmes de prise de décision et de contrôle dans les organisations.

Dans un premier temps l'étude présente quelques repères théoriques importants en la matière. Ce sont ensuite les niveaux et les objets du contrôle dans les organisations qui sont abordés, en relation avec les orientations stratégiques mises en oeuvre. Deux types d'organisation peuvent être caractérisés : l'organisation "fonctionnelle", classique, hiérarchisée (où les impulsions sont données et contrôlées du sommet de la hiérarchie) avec un système d'information et de communication conçu selon un schéma vertical, visant à minimiser les coûts opérationnels ; l'organisation "transversale", prenant en considération l'efficacité d'ensemble de l'organisation (pas fragmentée par fonction). Cette conception moderne de l'organisation privilégie les "processus" et les "activités" d'une entreprise. Interactivité, flexibilité, décentralisation, efficacité sont les mots clés, mais selon le modèle de Robert Simons ce sont aussi des comportements et des valeurs qui sont pris en considération. Les nouvelles technologies d'information et de communication (NICT) permettent de répondre aux nouvelles exigences de gestion des entreprises compétitives de la fin de ce siècle. L'auteur en apporte le témoignage en examinant les possibilités des logiciels intégrés, des technologies "GROUPWARE", des réseaux Inter- et Intranets, et des "magasins de données" ("data warehousing").

Zusammenfassung

Einfluß der neuen Informations- und Kommunikationstechnologien auf die Organisationskontrollsysteme

Die Unternehmen müssen mit ständigem Wandel umgehen. Die Informationstechnologien sind gleichzeitig Ursache und Mittel dieses Wandels, der sich besonders auf die Entscheidungsfindung und auf die Kontrolle innerhalb der Organisationen auswirkt.

Zunächst gibt die Studie einige in diesem Bereich wichtige theoretische Orientierungspunkte. Dann werden die Objekte der Kontrolle und die jeweilige Kontrollebene angesprochen und mit den strategischen Entscheidungen in Verbindung gebracht. Zwei Organisationsformen lassen sich dabei charakterisieren : eine "funktionelle", klassische, hierarchisierte, bei der die Anstöße von der Spitze der Hierarchie aus gegeben und kontrolliert werden, und zwar mittels eines vertikalen Kommunikationssystems, das die Reduzierung der Kosten bezweckt. Dann die "transversale" Organisation, welche die Effizienz der gesamten nicht in Funktionen gegliederten Organisationen zu berücksichtigen sucht. Diese modernere Organisationskonzeption hat in erster Linie Prozesse und Tätigkeiten im Auge. Interaktivität, Flexibilität, Dezentralisierung und Effizienz sind hier die Schlüsselbegriffe.

Doch gemäß dem Robert-Simons-Modell werden auch Verhaltensweisen und Werte berücksichtigt. Die neuen Informations und Kommunikationstechnologien (NIKT) sind eine Antwort auf die neuen Erfordernisse einer sich dem Wettbewerb dieses ausgehenden Jahrhunderts stellenden Betriebsführung. Der Autor belegt dies, indem er Softwarepakete, 'Groupeware'-Technologie, Inter- und Intranet sowie "Data-Warehousing" einbezieht.

References

ANTHONY, R. (1988): *The Management Control Function*. Boston. Harvard Business Press.

APPLEGATE, L./MCFARLAN, F.W./MCKENNEY, J. (1997): *Corporate Information Systems Management*. 4th edition. Irwin.

BRIOLE, A./CRAIPEAU, S./FAGUET-PICK, B. (1997): Groupware, contrôle et gestion des activités: le sens des convergences. *Actes du Colloque A.I.M.* Strasbourg. Mai.

CATS-BARIL, W./THOMPSON, R. (1997): *Information Technology and Management*. Irwin.

CHILD, J. (1987): Information Technology, Organization, and the Response to Strategic Challenges. *California Management Review*. Fall. pp. 33-50.

DE RONGÉ, Y./CERRADA, K. (1996): Impacts of the implementation of a new management information system on the management control of its subsidiaries by a European multinational: a case study. *Working paper* presented at the EAA Conference in Bergen. May.

FRANCES, J./GARNSEY, E. (1996): Supermarkets and suppliers in the United Kingdom: System Integration, Information and Control. *Accounting, Organizations and Society*. Vol. 21. N° 6. August. pp. 591-610.

GORRY, G./SCOTT-MORTON, M. (1971): A framework for management information systems. *Sloan Management Review*. GORRY, G./SCOTT-MORTON, M. (1989): *Sloan Management Review. Spring*. pp. 49-61.

HAMMER, M./CHAMPY (1993): *Reengineering the corporation*. Harper Business.

KELLY, S. (1996): *Data warehousing: the route to mass customization*. J. Wiley. Revised edition.

LORINO, P. (1995): *Comptes et récits de la performance*. Les Editions d'Organisation. Paris.

LORINO, P. (1996): Le déploiement de la valeur par les processus. *Revue française de gestion*. Juin-Juillet-Août.

LOWE, T./ PUXTY, T. (1989): The Problems of a Paradigm: A Critique of the Prevailing Orthodoxy in Management Control. in: W. Chua, T. Lowe and T. Puxty. *Critical Perspectives in Management Control*. London. MacMillan.

MACINTOSH, N. (1985): *The Social Software of Accounting and Information Systems*. J. Wiley. New-York.

MALONE, T. (1997): Is Empowerment Just a Fad? Control, Decision Making, and IT. *Sloan Management Review*. Winter. pp. 23-35.

MARKUS, L./ROBEY, D. (1988): Information Technology and Organizational Change: Causal Structure in Theory and Research. *Management Science*. Vol. 34. N° 5. May. pp. 583-598.

NOLAN, R./CROSON, D. (1995): *Creative Destruction*. Harvard Business School Press. Boston.

PERROW, C. (1967): A Framework for the Comparative Analysis of Organizations. *American Sociological Review*. April. pp. 194-208.

PORTER, M. (1980): *Competitive Strategy*. The Free Press.

PORTER, M. (1985): *Competitive Advantage: Creating and Sustaining Superior Performance*. The Free Press.

PRAX, J.Y. (1997): *Manager la connaissance dans l'entreprise*. Insep Editions. Paris.

REIX, R. (1990): L'impact organisationnel des nouvelles technologies de l'information. *Revue Française de Gestion*. Janvier-Février. pp. 100-106.

ROBEY, D. (1977): Computers and Management Structure: Some Empirical Findings Re-examined. *Human Relations*, 30. pp. 963-976.

SIMON, H. (1960): *The new science of management decision*. Harper & Row. New-York.

SIMONS, R. (1995): Control in an Age of Empowerment. *Harvard Business Review*. March-April. pp. 80-88.

SIMONS, R. (1994): *Levers of Control: How Managers Use Innovative Control Systems to Drive Strategic Renewal*. Harvard Business School Press.

Adamantios Diamantopoulos
and Anne L. Souchon

Information Utilisation by Exporting Firms: Conceptualisation, Measurement, and Impact on Export Performance

1.   Background

2.   Methodology
     A. Exploratory research
     B. Mail survey

3.   Dimensions of export information use

4.   Export information use and export performance

5.   Results and discussion

6.   Conclusions
     A. Managerial implications
     B. Future research

1.   Background

Relevant knowledge is critical to sound decision-making (Barabba, 1983), since *"a marketing policy is only as good as the information on which it is based"* (Tookey, 1964, p. 59). However, rather than mere acquisition, it is the *use* of information which ensures the success or failure of organisations (Glazer, 1991). This is because *"essentially the same information is available to competing firms at about the same time. As a consequence, competitive advantage is to be found increasingly in what is done with information, i.e., how it is used or employed rather than in who does or does not have it"* (Zaltman and Moorman, 1988, p. 16). Organisations which have learned to absorb, make sense of, and react quickly to, information tend to possess a deeper understanding of their markets (Day and Glazer, 1994). Such an understanding assists in the creation of superior customer value and the identification of a sustainable competitive advantage (Narver and Slater, 1990). In turn, firms which have adopted such market-oriented principles are likely to benefit from enhanced organisational performance (Jaworski and Kohli, 1993).

With the growing importance of marketing information to business success (Barabba and Zaltman, 1991), the study of information use has increased in recent years. Indeed, as early as 1979, marketing information use became the focus of a major piece of research by the special joint commission of the American Marketing Association and the Marketing Science Institute. In the 1990s, the concept of information use remained a topical issue as evidenced by its inclusion in the Marketing Science Institute's *List of Research Priorities 1990-1992.*

Although the phrase "information use" appears to warrant no clarification since it conjures up a straightforward concept, it is not so simple a term (Beyer and Trice, 1982; Larsen, 1985). Indeed, knowledge utilisation is a complex construct, which must be defined before it can be studied empirically (Larsen, 1981). Information use has been defined as *"taking research into account"* (Weiss and Bucavalas, 1977, p. 214), the *"interpretation and analysis of information"* (Goldstein and Zack, 1989, p. 314), and *"the extent to which the research influences the user's decision making"* (Moorman et al., 1992, p. 316). Synthesising these definitions, it can be said that information utilisation is the process by which information is considered when decisions are made.

Over the past two decades, a number of authors have attempted to conceptualise information use (e.g., Conner, 1981; Havelock, 1986; Taylor, 1991; Slater and Narver, 1995). The most common classification of information use is along an *instrumental* and a *conceptual* dimension, and is generally first credited to Caplan et al. (1975). Instrumental use of information has been defined as the direct application of information to solve a specific problem or to make a particular decision (e.g., Deshpandé and Zaltman, 1982). For example, *"when a decision to introduce a new product is based on marketing research findings and recommendations, we have an instance of instrumental use of knowledge"* (Menon and Varadarajan, 1992, p. 55). Conceptual use refers to the indirect application of information, in the sense that information is used to broaden the managerial knowledge base without serving any one particular project (e.g., Moorman, 1995). Conceptual use also encompasses future use of information (Rich, 1977). Knorr (1977) also identified a symbolic type of information use with three main variants. The first one occurs when information is distorted in order to support the decision-maker's opinion in the eyes of his/her subordinates, colleagues and superiors (e.g., Goodman, 1993). The second type of symbolic use is an instance where information is used to justify a decision made previously (e.g., Feldman and March, 1981). The third type of symbolic use occurs when information is used merely to ensure good relationships with information providers (Menon and Varadarajan, 1992).

A separate perspective on information use is that of *extent* as opposed to *type* of use (Souchon and Diamantopoulos, 1996). Though extent of information use could potentially be captured by the extent to which information is used instrumentally, conceptually and symbolically, Weiss (1981) proposes that extent of information use is best captured by the number of people or functional areas within the organisation who use information. This perspective is thus complementary to the type of information use that occurs, as reflected in the relative reliance on instrumental, conceptual and symbolic use.

The current study focuses on *export* information use. In an export setting, the importance of effective information use is highlighted by the fact that *"competitive competence rests in a major way on a firm's level of export-related skill, the learning that takes place and the knowledge that flows from it"* (Seringhaus, 1988, p. 100). Given the unfamiliar international environment which exporters face, export performance has been shown to be affected by extensive international market information (e.g., Koh et al., 1993). Whether in a domestic or an export context, empirical evidence of the effects of information use on organisational performance is scant, as most studies have focused on the *antecedents* of information utilisation (e.g., Deshpandé and Zaltman, 1982). Studies which have explicitly considered *outcomes of,* as opposed to influences on, information use are scarce. O'Reilly (1978) who investigated, in a laboratory experiment, the impact of intentional information distortion (i.e., symbolic use) on job satisfaction and individual and group performance, found negative linkages. Moorman (1995) examined the relationships between instrumental and conceptual information use, and new product decision outcomes. She found beneficial effects of both information use dimensions on her outcome measure. The latter captured new product performance (e.g., market share relative to its stated objective), timeliness (e.g., well-timed versus poorly timed), and creativity (e.g., whether the new product spawned ideas for other products).

The literature on information use is short of *empirical* studies reporting the outcomes of information utilisation, despite a plethora of *conceptual* articles praising the latter's beneficial effect on decision-making (Barabba, 1983), and ultimately on company performance (e.g., Goodman, 1993). Indeed, a large number of authors caution against using information in a manner which could be described as political (e.g., Feldman and March, 1981; Connolly and Thorn, 1987; Goodman, 1993), and advocate a more systematic and objective use of information (e.g., Tushman and Nadler, 1978; Schoemaker and Russo, 1993; Moorman, 1995).

In the light of the above, the objectives of the present paper are threefold. The first objective is to determine the *dimensions* of information use which are applicable in an export context. The second objective is to develop psychometrically sound multi-item *measures* of export information use; while it is generally accepted that information use is a multi-dimensional construct, only one of those dimensions has been operationalised in previous measures (see Deshpandé and Zaltman, 1982). The final objective is to examine the effect of different types of export information use on export *performance*. Taken collectively, the results of the study should assist in determining *how* export information should be best put to use, with obvious implications for exporters.

2. Methodology

A. Exploratory research

A recent review of the literature has shown that the topic of export information use is as yet virtually unexplored (see Souchon and Diamantopoulos, 1996). Although Hart et al. (1994) consider the construct in their study of export marketing research, their primary focus is upon the extent of export information use, ignoring its different dimensions. Similarly, Diamantopoulos and Horncastle (1996), though in a sense pioneers of the study of export information use, adopt a narrow perspective by concentrating exclusively on export marketing research information and a single dimension of use (instrumental use). In short, the construct of export information use has not, to date, been thoroughly investigated. Bearing in mind that exploratory research is particularly necessary when little is known about a phenomenon (Churchill, 1996) and when no reliable and valid quantitative measures of a construct exist (Patton, 1980), in-depth qualitative interviews were initially conducted with export managers in UK firms. The objectives of this preliminary research were as follows:

– to identify the dimensions of information use in an export setting,

- to develop a pool of items, which, together with items drawn from the literature, could be used to capture the information use dimensions uncovered, and
- to complement the literature for the development of hypotheses linking export information use to export performance.

The collected interview material was subsequently analysed using the methods advocated by Miles and Huberman (1994); full details of this stage of the research can be found in Diamantopoulos and Souchon (1996).

B.   Mail survey

The second stage in the research involved a cross-sectional survey of export companies using a questionnaire developed on the basis of the literature and the exploratory research phase. The questionnaire was pretested using 200 exporting companies in the UK in two separate pilot tests, and modified as a result. In the main survey, manufacturing exporters were randomly selected from a sampling frame obtained from Dun & Bradstreet. After the initial mailing and follow-up procedure, an effective response rate of 24 percent was obtained. The response rate achieved in the present study is comparable to other information use studies. For example, Schlegelmilch and Therivel's (1988) survey of marketing research usage among UK firms achieved a response rate of 27 percent, while Schleglmilch et al's (1993) study of export marketing research reported a 33 percent response rate.

3.   Dimensions of export information use

Probably the most common conceptualisation of information use is the two-fold classification encompassing instrumental and conceptual use (Caplan et al., 1975). However, in the late 1970s and early 1980s, the contention arose that conceptual use was far more widespread than instrumental use (e.g., Rich, 1977; and Weiss, 1977, 1981). To illustrate this point, Deshpandé (1981) concluded that knowledge tends to be used more for its ability to provide enlightenment to decision-makers rather than for its capacity to directly guide decisions. This, in turn, led to the two-fold classification being heavily criticised. For example, Dunn (1986) posited that instrumental use was not a separate dimension of information use, but rather, a particular type of conceptual use. According to this view, instrumental and conceptual use of information *"cannot be juxtaposed as if they were mutually exclusive; nor can they be arranged along a continuum whose poles occupy the same level of analysis"* (Dunn, 1986, p. 336).

The exploratory study also revealed that, in an export context, instrumental and conceptual use of information are not easily distinguishable, thus lending support to Dunn's (1986) contention that the two dimensions cannot be dissociated. The analysis of the in-depth interviews (see Diamantopoulos and Souchon, 1996) showed conceptual use on the same network of linkages as instrumental use, implying an association between the two dimensions of use. In addition, conceptual use, which was often described in terms of future use, appeared to represent specific and direct information use (but in the future, as opposed to immediately). Together with previous contentions that instrumental and conceptual uses are, in fact, only one dimension (e.g., Weiss, 1977; Dunn, 1986), the interview finding suggest a framework of export information use, with (a) an instrumental/conceptual, and (b) a symbolic dimension of the construct.

When examining export information issues, it is important to consider sources of information which are likely to determine both the extent of information collection (McAuley, 1993) and the type of information use (Souchon and Diamantopoulos, 1997). It is thus argued that sources of export information will be crucial in explaining *why* information is used in specific ways (i.e., either instrumentally/conceptually or symbolically). Sources of export information can be classified into three broad acquisition modes, namely export marketing research, export assistance, and export market intelligence (Souchon and Diamantopoulos, 1996). Export marketing research is a formal and structured information gathering mechanism (Douglas and Craig, 1983) which encompasses in-house marketing research departments, independent outside agencies, and syndicated research (e.g., Sinkula, 1994). It has been argued that export marketing research is less rigorous, less formal, less precise and less quantitative than domestic marketing research (e.g., Cavusgil, 1984). Export assistance refers to information services provided by official, non-marketing research, organisations, such as government departments, embassies, banks, exporters' associations. It includes both standardised and customised information provision (Seringhaus, 1985). Finally, export market intelligence is the process of gathering information informally in the course of day-to-day activities. For example, visits to export customers will be such a source of useful information (e.g., Denis and Depelteau, 1985), as will attending international trade fairs (e.g., Kleinschmidt and Ross, 1984).

Established measure development procedures were employed to develop reliable and valid measures of each dimension of export information use (for full details, see Diamantopoulos and Souchon, 1997). Measures of export information use were first developed on the basis of export market intelligence information and then replicated onto comparable scales of export marketing research and export assistance information. Appendices 1 and 2 list the specific items employed to capture instrumental/conceptual and symbolic use of export information, while Table 1 provides descriptive statistics on the derived scales.

Table 1: Summary statistics of export information use scales

	Instrumental/conceptual			Symbolic		
	EMR	EA	EMI	EMR	EA	EMI
Number of Cases	92	111	168	93	113	168
Number of Items	12	12	12	11	11	11
Cronbach α	.78	.80	.80	.73	.75	.73
Mean	42.90	40.37	43.42	26.91	26.73	28.17
Standard Deviation	5.80	5.96	6.07	5.19	5.09	5.31
Average Inter-Item Correlation	.23	.26	.26	.20	.22	.20
Average Item-Whole Correlation	.43	.45	.45	.38	.40	.38

EMR = export marketing research, EA = export assistance, EMI = export market intelligence

In addition to being internally consistent (see Table 1), the six scales of export information use were all found to possess high content, convergent, discriminant, and nomological validity. Content validity was ensured by drawing each item from the literature or from the in-depth interviews conducted with export decision-makers. Furthermore, every aspect of each dimension of export information use was included in the relevant scale, often captured by more than one item (see Appendices 1 and 2). Convergent validity was assessed by correlating each instrumental/conceptual use scale with the other two instrumental/conceptual use scales, and by correlating each symbolic use scale with the other two symbolic use scales (validity). In addition, the scales pertaining to export marketing research information were correlated to the scales pertaining to symbolic use (discriminant validity). It was found that all three instrumental/conceptual use scales were strongly and positively correlated, and all three symbolic use scales were also highly positively related. In contrast, the correlations testing for discriminant validity were, as expected, either negative or not significant. Finally, nomological validity was assessed by correlating the six export information use scales with export information acquisition, export information overload, non-use, immediate use and future use of export information. Ninety two percent of the postulated correlations were found to be statistically significant at $p < .05$ and in the expected direction.

Extent of use was also captured using a multi-item measure. Specifically, extent of use was measured on a five-point frequency scale indicating the extent to which various functional areas (namely export, marketing, finance, production, R&D, and top management) use export information. The six items were subsequently summed up to create an index of "intra-organisational" use.

4. Export information use and export performance

Proper use of information can assist in the identification of opportunities and threats (e.g., Moorman, 1995) and thus help to resolve marketing problems (e.g., Barabba and Zaltman, 1991). Export information, however, does not solely concern the export function of companies; for instance, R&D personnel may use export information in the development of specific export products and/or the adaptation of existing products for export markets. It is, therefore, expected that the more functional areas have access to, and make use of export information, the better the export decisions (and, as a direct result, the export performance) will be.

H_1:   *Intra-organisational use will be positively related to export performance.*

In the context of marketing research, Hooley and West (1984, p. 347) state that *"those companies with zero or low usage could significantly improve their performance by making better use of marketing research"*. Similarly, Hart and Diamantopoulos (1993, p. 69) claim that *"even if the quality of marketing research information itself is good, unless it is put to good use by the manager(s) concerned, then it is unlikely to have an impact on the decision-making process and, ultimately, on performance"*. Finally, Moorman (1995) uncovered positive relationships between instrumental and conceptual use of information, and the effectiveness of new product decisions. Given the benefits of using marketing research (e.g., Hooley and West, 1984) and the importance of "good" use of information (e.g., Tushman and Nadler, 1978), it is proposed that:

H_2:   *Instrumental/conceptual use of export marketing research information will be positively related to export performance.*

However, the case of instrumental/conceptual use of export assistance information may be different. In their exploratory study of UK exporters, Diamantopoulos and Souchon (1996) found that export assistance was regarded by decision-makers as providing information of poor quality. If this is the case, then decisions actually based on this information are unlikely to contribute to export success. Moreover, export assistance is often accused of providing information that is too general to satisfy decision-making needs (e.g., Reid, 1984), which implies that the risk of making poor decisions based on this information will be high (Glazer et al., 1992). Based on these considerations, it is expected that:

H₃: *Instrumental/conceptual use of export assistance information will be negatively related to export performance.*

Export market intelligence, especially in the form of face-to-face personal communication, tends to be exporters' favourite source of information (e.g., Reid, 1984; McAuley, 1993). In a recent study, Diamantopoulos and Souchon (1996) revealed that export managers trusted export market intelligence information because it emanated directly from the market place. Thus it would appear that export market intelligence provides "good" information. Consequently, when put to "good" use, such information would be expected to enhance the quality of the decisions made. Hence, it is anticipated that:

H₄: *Instrumental/conceptual use of export market intelligence information will be positively related to export performance.*

Symbolic use of information entails the making of decisions based upon instinct and/or the use of information merely to support these decisions (Menon and Varadarajan, 1992). However, decisions based upon instinct are likely to be very risky and error-prone (Schoemaker and Russo, 1993). Indeed, in an export setting, Crick et al. (1994) found that companies which used export information to back up hunches tended to be lower performing firms, as compared to companies using information in a more instrumental manner. Consequently, it is expected that:

H₅: *Symbolic use of export information (from any source) will be negatively related to export performance.*

Table 2 summarises the hypotheses to be tested.

To operationalise export performance, a variety of measures was used as recommended by Shoham (1991), Madsen (1989), and Mathyssens and Pauwels (1996) among others. A full listing of the measures employed can be found in Appendix 3.

Table 2: Hypotheses linking export information use to export performance

Use dimensions	Hypotheses	Anticipated Relationship with Export Performance
Intra-organisational use	H_1	+
Instrumental/conceptual use of EMR	H_2	+
Instrumental/conceptual use of EA	H_3	-
Instrumental/conceptual use of EMI	H_4	+
Symbolic use	H_5	-

EMR = export marketing research, EA = export assistance, EMI = export market intelligence

4. Results and discussion

In order to test the hypotheses linking export information use to export performance, both Pearson and Spearman correlations were employed. Specifically, where variables were not normally distributed (as evidenced by a histogram and a Kolmogorov-Smirnov test), Spearman correlations were employed. Where the variables tended to be normally distributed, Pearson correlations were used. The results of the analysis are presented in Table 3. Note that only significant coefficients are shown (at $p<.10$ or better, one-tailed significance).

Intra-organisational use of export information is highly beneficial to export performance, since eight out of 10 correlations were found to be positive and significant at $p<.05$. This finding indicates that export information should be disseminated within exporting companies so that it can be used by functional areas other than export or marketing departments (see also Diamantopoulos and Cadogan, 1996). The benefits of intra-organisational use are likely to be two-fold. First, as already noted, the quality of export-related decision making within the firm is likely to be enhanced if different functions have access to export information. Second, as intra-organisational use increases, symbolic use of export information decreases. This is evidenced by the negative correlations between intra-organisational use and symbolic use of export marketing research ($r = -.29$), export assistance ($r = -.15$), and export market intelligence ($r = -.10$)

Table 3: Hypothesis testing results

	Export sales		Export growth (3-year)		Competitive performance		Satisfaction with performance		Overall performance	
	per employee	per country	sales (%)	profit (%)	market position	relative performance	raw	weighted	overall perception	index
Intra-organisational use										
	.37	.23	.18		.24	.28	.19		.28	.38
Instrumental/Conceptual use										
EMR				-.14			-.25	-.21		
EA	-.17				-.19					
EMI	.18	.24			.18	.33	.22	.22	.23	.22
Symbolic use										
EMR			-.18			-.32				
EA		-.13								
EMI		-.12	-.15			-.22			-.12	-.13

EMR : Export marketing research
EA : Export assistance
EMI : Export market intelligence

respectively. Given that symbolic use of export information involves counter-rational behaviour (see also below), it is likely that a means of reducing such behaviour (such as a company culture conducive to intra-organisational use of export information) will enhance export performance.

Contrary to expectations, instrumental/conceptual use of export marketing research information appears to have a detrimental effect on export performance (though mainly on the satisfaction indicators). An explanation for this finding may lie in the *quality* of the information provided by export marketing research bodies. Indeed it has been argued that export marketing research lacks in formality, rigour, precision and objectivity compared to its domestic counterpart (e.g., Cavusgil, 1984, 1985). If this is the case, then the quality of the supplied information may be suspect leading to sub-optimal decisions. Where export assistance information is concerned, the anticipated negative relationship between instrumental/conceptual use of the latter and export performance was partially supported. Specifically, instrumental/conceptual use of export assistance was found to be negatively correlated with both export sales per employee and competitive market position. Eight out of ten correlations between export performance and instrumental/conceptual use of export market intelligence were found to be positive and significant. It would thus appear that using export market intelligence in an instrumental/conceptual manner will be a most effective means of enhancing export performance.

The hypothesis pertaining to a negative relationship between symbolic use and export performance was partially supported in the context of export marketing research information. Specifically, symbolic use of export marketing research was found to be negatively correlated to growth in sales and to export performance in relation to competitors' export performance. With regards to symbolic use of export assistance, only one negatively significant linkage was uncovered (with export sales per country). While this provides only weak support for hypothesis H_5, a possible explanation is that UK exporters may not trust this type of information and thus may not acquire it to any great extent (Diamantopoulos and Souchon, 1996). As a result, there may be too little export assistance information available to the decision-maker to significantly affect export performance. Finally, symbolic use of export market intelligence information was found to be largely negatively related to export performance, corroborating the expected negative link between symbolic use and performance.

5. Conclusions

A. Managerial implications

Intra-organisational use of export information was found to enhance export performance. The more people/departments in the organisation put export information to use, the more decisions will be based on information; consequently, the quality of the decisions made is likely to increase, resulting in enhanced performance. Closer examination of intra-organisational use also revealed that this use was negatively related to symbolic use of information, suggesting that when export information is disseminated across functional areas and used by people from various departments, symbolic use is reduced. The use of export information intra-organisationally thus appears to be doubly beneficial, because (a) more decisions are based on information, and (b) less symbolic use of information is likely to take place.

In the context of export marketing research, both instrumental/conceptual and symbolic use were found to be detrimental to export performance. The first finding is highly surprising and counter-intuitive, and may suggest that export marketing research information is lacking in quality. Consequently, direct implementation in the making of export decisions would result in poor decisions if such information were to be unreliable or outdated. Given the relatively high costs of export market research (Douglas and Craig, 1993), careful evaluation of the quality of any research commissioned/undertaken is necessary to ensure that export decision makers are getting value for their money. As far as the negative impact of symbolic use is concerned, this is consistent with expectations and reflects the fact that distortion and/or manipulation of export information is likely to hinder the decision making process.

Instrumental/conceptual use of export assistance was also found to be negatively related to two export performance indicators, a finding which also raises questions regarding the quality of such information (c.f. Diamantopoulos et al., 1993). On the other hand, instrumental/conceptual use of export market intelligence information was found to exert a positive influence upon export performance. This latter finding is particularly important since informal sources of information are often favoured by decision-makers and thought to be relevant and accurate (Saunders and Jones, 1990).

Bearing the above in mind, it can be argued that the detrimental effect of instrumental/conceptual use of export marketing research and export assistance information may not be due to this type of use being "bad", but may be a manifestation of "good" use of "bad" (i.e. poor quality) information. This explanation would appear to be supported by the exploratory findings which highlighted that (a) marketing research information was not perceived to be as useful as intelligence information because it is not collected by actual "players" in the relevant industry, but by independent observers (e.g., market research agencies), and (b) export assistance bodies were often perceived to provide information that was too general for the specific needs of individual exporters and/or out-dated (Diamantopoulos and Souchon, 1996). In conclusion, exporters should be encouraged to collect export market intelligence information since this information appears to be the key to their export success. Once it has been acquired, such information should be used instrumentally/conceptually (applied directly in the making of specific export decisions). Export intelligence information should also be preserved to be used in more than one decision by more than one individual. It should be widely disseminated within the firm so that different functions/departments can access it; such intraorganisational use also impacts favourably on export performance.

B.   Future research

Jobber and Elliott (1992) indicate that research findings are likely to be judged more favourably in successful companies than in unsuccessful ones. Particularly in the context of the fast moving consumer goods sector, organisations often attribute past product failures to unreliable market research information, and therefore become wary of making decisions based upon research reports. Conversely, when a company is successful it is more likely to have faith in marketing research (Jobber and Elliott, 1992). Given that a positive evaluation of information is linked to a greater extent of information utilisation (Menon and Varadarajan, 1992), the level of overall company performance is likely to affect the level of information use within that company. A longitudinal study would be appropriate in establishing the causal order involved (Katsikeas, 1994), since this cannot be determined from a cross-sectional survey. In a longitudinal study, the researcher may be able to *directly* observe the *changes* in export performance attributed to specific uses of export information. For instance, in the making of a particular decision, symbolic use of export marketing research information may have been involved. On subsequent measurement of the firm's export performance, a deterioration of the latter may be observed, which may then be directly attributed to poor information use (or, alternatively, use of poor information).

Future research should also pay attention to developing a measure of information *quality*. Such a measure would be particularly useful in explaining why certain types of information are used in a certain way, and clarify the relationship between information use and export performance. In this study, the quality of the information provided by the three export information sources was not captured. Had such a measure been included, the negative relationship between instrumental/conceptual use of export marketing research information and export performance could have been subjected to further scrutiny.

In order to further interpret the findings of this study, post-survey in-depth interviews ought to be conducted. This approach would be quite different to the exploratory approach adopted in the preliminary phase of this study. Rather than seeking to gain insights into the construct of export information use, the focus would be on explaining the findings uncovered in the survey. For example, one could examine why exporters use export marketing research, even when such use impacts negatively on their export performance.

Finally, the findings of this study reveal that export market intelligence is of utmost importance to exporters as instrumental/conceptual use of this information clearly enhances export performance. The information sources belonging to this acquisition mode are mainly personal contact sources (e.g., with customers, suppliers etc.). The relationship marketing literature may thus provide additional insights into the manner in which such contacts or relationships can be established and maintained so as to maximise their information generation potential.

Résumé

Utilisation de l'information par les entreprises exportatrices : conceptualisation, mesure et impact sur la performance

Dans le domaine du marketing il est désormais admis que ce n'est pas l'acquisition de l'information - ou en d'autres termes la quantité ou la qualité de l'information disponible - qui conditionne la performance d'une entreprise, mais bien l'utilisation qu'elle en fait. Ce chapitre explore plus particulièrement le problème de la mise en valeur de l'information à des fins de gestion de l'exportation, ce qui est une préoccupation nouvelle dans la littérature.

Au plan conceptuel une distinction est proposée entre l'usage instrumental et l'usage symbolique de l'information. Le premier relève d'une démarche rationnelle d'utilisation de l'information pour fonder les décisions prises en matière d'exportation. Le second ("symbolique") concerne une démarche "politique" c'est-à-dire que l'information est utilisée, voire déformée, manipulée, pour justifier des décisions déjà prises ou assurer de bonnes relations avec des partenaires.

L'étude s'appuie sur une étude empirique décrivant le comportement face à l'information d'exportateurs britanniques (large échantillon constitué à partir des données de Dun & Bradstreet). Dans le cadre conceptuel retenu (instrumental/symbolique), une méthode de mesure est décrite, suivie par l'analyse de six hypothèses concernant la relation entre l'utilisation de l'information (à des fins de veille commerciale, de recherche marketing ou de décision-marketing) et la performance à l'exportation. Les résultats obtenus sont discutés du point de vue de leur implication managériale ainsi que de leur portée scientifique.

Adamantios DIAMANTOPOULOS and Anne L. SOUCHON

Zusammenfassung

Die Nutzung von Informationen in exportorientierten Unternehmen: Konzeptualisierung, Messung und Folgen für die Leistungsfähigkeit

Im Bereich des Marketings gilt es inzwischen als erwiesen, daß weniger die Informationsakquisition – mit anderen Worten die Menge und Qualität verfügbarer Daten - die Leistung eines Unternehmens bedingen, sondern vielmehr das, was es daraus macht. Dieser Beitrag widmet sich der Frage nach der Aufbereitung der Informationen zum Zwecke des Ausfuhrmanagements. Dies ist in der Fachliteratur ein neuer Untersuchungsgegenstand.

Auf der Begriffsebene unterscheidet man - neueren Vorschlägen folgend - zwischen instrumentellem und symbolischem Gebrauch der Informationen. Der erste Begriff bezieht sich auf ein rationelles Verwendungsschema zur Absicherung der Entscheidungsfindung im Export. Der zweite (symbolische) betrifft ein strategisches und methodisches Vorgehen, d.h. daß die Informationen benutzt oder auch verzerrt und manipuliert werden im Hinblick auf schon getroffene Entscheidungen oder zur Sicherung guter Zusammenarbeit mit den Partnerfirmen.

Der Beitrag beruht auf einer empirischen Untersuchung, in der die Nutzung von Informationen in britischen Exportfirmen beschrieben wird (breite, auf Material von de Dun & Bradstreet basierende Stichprobe). Im gegebenen (instrumental/symbolisch) Begriffsrahmen wird eine Meßmethode beschrieben. Es folgt die Analyse von sechs Hypothesen, in der das Verhältnis untersucht wird zwischen der Nutzung von Informationen (zum Zweck der Handelsüberwachung, der Marketingforschung oder für Marketingentscheidungen) und der Leistungsfähigkeit im Export. Die Ergebnisse der Studie werden dann im Hinblick auf ihre Konsequenzen für Management und Wissenschaft hin erörtert.

References

BARABBA, V.P. (1983): Making Use of Methodologies Developed in Academia: Lessons from One Practitioner's Experience. in: R. Kilmann et al. (eds.): *Producing Useful Knowledge for Organizations*. New-York. Praeger Publishers.

BARABBA, V.P./ZALTMAN, G. (1991): *Hearing the Voice of the Market - Competitive Advantage Through Creative Use of Market Information*. Harvard Business School Press. Boston. Massachusetts.

BEYER, J.M./TRICE, H.M. (1982): The Utilization Process: A Conceptual Framework and Synthesis of Empirical Findings. *Administrative Science Quarterly* 27. 591-622.

CAPLAN, N./MORRISON, A./STAMBAUGH, R.J. (1975): *The Use of Social Science Knowledge in Policy Decisions at the National Level*. Ann Arbor. MI: Institute for Social Research.

CAVUSGIL, S.T (1984): International Marketing Research: Insights Into Company Practices. *Research in Marketing* 7. 261-288.

CAVUSGIL, S.T. (1985): Guidelines for EMR. *Business Horizons*. November-December. 27-33.

CAVUSGIL, S.T./ZOU, S. (1994): Marketing Strategy-Performance Relationship: An Investigation of the Empirical Link in Export Market Ventures. *Journal of Marketing* 58. January. 1-21.

CHURCHILL, G.A. (1996): *Marketing Research: Methodological Foundations*. The Dryden Press International Edition.

CONNER, R.F. (1981): Measuring Evaluation Utilization: A Critique of Different Techniques. in: J.A. Ciarlo (ed.): *Utilizing Evaluation: Concepts and Measurement Techniques*. Beverly Hills, CA. Sage Publication. 59-75.

CONNOLLY, T./THORN, B. (1987): Predecisional Information Acquisition: Effects of Task Variables on Suboptimal Search Strategies. *Organizational Behavior and Human Decision Processes* 39. 397-417.

CRICK, D./JONES, M./HART, S. (1994): International Marketing Research Activities of UK Exporters: An Exploratory Study. *Journal of Euromarketing* 3. N° 2. 7-26.

DAY, G./GLAZER, R. (1994): Harnessing the Marketing Information Revolution: Toward the Market-Driven Learning Organization. in: R.C. Blattberg/ R. Glazer/J.D.C. Little (eds.): *The Marketing Information Revolution*. Harvard Business School Press. Boston. Massachusetts.

DENIS, J.E./DEPELTEAU, D. (1985): Market Knowledge, Diversification and Export Expansion. *Journal of International Business Studies*. Fall. 77-89.

DESHPANDE, R. (1981): Action and Enlightenment Functions of Research. *Knowledge: Creation, Diffusion, Utilization* 2. N° 3. March. 317-330.

DESHPANDE, R./ZALTMAN, G. (1982): Factors Affecting the Use of Market Research Information: A Path Analysis. *Journal of Marketing Research* 19. 14-31.

DIAMANTOPOULOS, A./CADOGAN, J.W. (1996): Internationalizing the Market Orientation Construct: An In-Depth Interview Approach. *Journal of Strategic Marketing* 4. 23-52.

DIAMANTOPOULOS, A./HORNCASTLE, S. (1996): Use of Export Marketing Research by Industrial Firms: An Application of Deshpandé and Zaltman's Model. *International Marketing Review.*

DIAMANTOPOULOS, A./SOUCHON, A.L. (1996): Instrumental, Conceptual and Symbolic Use of Export Information: An Exploratory Study of UK Firms. in: Cavusgil, S.T. (ed.): *Advances in International Marketing* 8. 117-144. Greenwich, CT. Jai Press Inc.

DIAMANTOPOULOS, A./SOUCHON, A.L. (1997): Measuring Export Information Use: Scale Development and Validation. in: *Marketing across Borders.* Proceedings of the Academy of Marketing (AM) & American Marketing Association (AMA). Manchester, UK. July 7. 139-155.

DOUGLAS, S.P./CRAIG, C.S. (1983): *International Marketing Research.* Prentice Hall.

DUNN, W.N. (1986): Conceptualizing Knowledge Use. in: G.M. Beal et al. (eds.): *Knowledge Generation, Exchange, and Utilization.* Boulder. Westview Press.

FELDMAN, M.S./MARCH, J.G. (1981): Information in Organizations as Signal and Symbol. *Administrative Science Quarterly* 26. 171-186.

GLAZER, R. (1991): Marketing in an Information-Intensive Environment: Strategic Implications of Knowledge as an Asset. Journal of Marketing 55. October. 1-19.

GLAZER, R./STECKEL, J.H./WINER, R.S. (1992): Locally Rational Decision Making: The Distracting Effect of Information on Managerial Performance. *Management Science* 38. February. 212-226.

GOLDSTEIN, D.K./ZACK, M.H. (1989): The Impact of Marketing Information Supply on Product Managers: An Organizational Information Processing Perspective. *Office: Technology and People* 4. N° 4. 313-336.

GOODMAN S.K. (1993): Information Needs for Management Decision-Making. *Records Management Quarterly* 27. N° 4. 12-23.

HART, S./DIAMANTOPOULOS, A. (1993): Marketing Research Activity and Company Performance: Evidence from Manufacturing Industry. *European Journal of Marketing* 27. N° 5. 54-72.

HART, S./WEBB, J.R./JONES, M.V. (1994): Export Marketing Research and the Effect of Export Experience in Industrial SMEs. *International Marketing Review* 11. N° 6. 4-22.

HAVELOCK, R.G. (1986): The Knowledge Perspective: Definition and Scope of a New Study Domain. in: Beal et al. (eds.): *Knowledge Generation, Exchange, and Utilization*. Westview Press Inc.

HOOLEY, G.J./WEST, C.J. (1984): The Untapped Markets for Marketing Research. *Journal of the Market Research Society* 26. October. 335-352.

JAWORSKI, B.J./KOHLI, A.J. (1993): Market Orientation: Antecedents and Consequences. *Journal of Marketing* 57. July. 53-70.

JOBBER, D./ELLIOTT, R.H. (1992): The Evaluation and Use of Marketing Research Information: A Behavioural Simulation. in: J. Whitelock et al. (eds): *Marketing Education Group Proceedings*.

KATSIKEAS, C.S. (1994): Export Competitive Advantages: The Relevance of Firm Characteristics. *International Marketing Review* 11. N° 3. 33-53.

KLEINSCHMIDT, E.J./ROSS, R.E. (1984): Export Performance and Foreign Market Information: Relationships for Small High-Technology Firms. *Canadian Journal of Small Business and Entrepreneurship* 2. N° 4. 8-23.

KNORR, K.D. (1977): Policymakers' Use of Social Science Knowledge: Symbolic or Instrumental? in: C. H. Weiss. (ed.): *Using Social Research in Public Policy Making*. Lexington Books. D. C. Heath and Company.

KOH, A.C./CHOW, J./SMITTIVATE, S. (1993): The Practice of International Marketing Research by Thai Exporters. *Journal of Global Marketing* 7. N° 2. 7-26.

LARSEN, J.K. (1981): Knowledge Utilization: Current Issues. in: R.F. Rich. (ed.): *The knowledge Cycle*. Beverly Hills, CA. Sage.

LARSEN, J.K. (1985): Effect of Time on Information Utilization. *Knowledge: Creation, Diffusion, Utilization* 7. N° 2. 143-159.

MCAULEY, A. (1993): The Perceived Usefulness of Export Information Sources. *European Journal of Marketing*. 52-64.

MENON, A./VARADARAJAN, R. (1992): A Model of Marketing Knowledge Use Within Firms. *Journal of Marketing* 56. 53-71.

MILES, M.B./HUBERMAN, A.M. ( ): *An Expanded Sourcebook: Qualitative Data Analysis*. Sage Publications.

MOORMAN, C. (1995): Organizational Market Information Processes: Cultural Antecedents and New Product Outcomes. *Journal of Marketing Research* 32. August. 318-335.

MOORMAN, C./ZALTMAN, G./DESHPANDE, R. (1992): Relationships Between Providers and Users of Market Research: The Dynamics of Trust Within and Between Organizations. *Journal of Marketing Research* 24. 314-328.

NARVER, J.C./SLATER, S.F. (1990): The Effect of Market Orientation on Business Profitability. *Journal of Marketing* 54. October. 20-35.

NUNNALLY, J.C. (1978): *Psychometric Theory*. McGraw-Hill Book Company. New-York.

O'REILLY, C.A. (1978): The Intentional Distortion of Information in Organizational Communication: A Laboratory and Field Investigation. *Human Relations* 31. N° 2. 173-193.

PATTON, M.Q. (1980): *Qualitative Evaluation Methods*. Beverly Hills, CA. Sage Publications.

REID, S.D. (1984): Information Acquisition and Export Entry Decisions in Small Firms. *Journal of Business Research* 12. 141-157.

RICH, R.F. (1977): Uses of Social Science Information by Federal Bureaucrats: Knowledge for Action versus Knowledge for Understanding. in: C.H. Weiss (ed.): *Using Social Research in Public Policy Making*. Lexington Books. D. C. Heath and Company.

SAUNDERS, C./JONES, J.W. (1990): Temporal Sequences in Information Acquisition for Decision Making: A Focus on Source and Medium. *Academy of Management Review* 15. N° 1. 29-46.

SCHLEGELMILCH, B.B./THERIVEL, S. (1988): The Use of Marketing Research in Engineering Companies: Empirical Evidence from the U.S. and the U.K. *Advances in Business Marketing* 3. 249-291.

SCHOEMAKER, P.J.H./RUSSO, J.E. (1993): A Pyramid of Decision Approaches. *California Management Review*. Fall. 9-31.

SERINGHAUS, R.F.H. (1985): How do Major Industrial Countries Support Firms' International Efforts. *ASAC Conference*. Université du Québec à Montréal.

SERINGHAUS, R.F.H. (1988): Export Knowledge, Strategy and Performance. *Developments in Marketing Science* 10. 97-101.

SINKULA, J.M. (1990): Perceived Characteristics, Organizational Factors, and the Utilization of External Market Research Suppliers. *Journal of Business Research*. August. 1-17.

SINKULA, J.M. (1994): Market Information Processing and Organizational Learning. *Journal of Marketing* 58. N° 1. 35-45.

SLATER, S.F./NARVER, J.C. (1995): Market Orientation and the Learning Organization. *Journal of Marketing* 59. July. 63-74.

DE SOLLA PRICE, D. (1975): Some Aspects of 'World Brain' Notions. in: M. Kochen (ed.): *Information for Action*. Academic Press. N.Y.

SOUCHON, A.L./DIAMANTOPOULOS, A. (1996): A Conceptual Framework of Export Information Use: Key Issues and Research Propositions. *Journal of International Marketing* 4. N° 3. 49-71.

SOUCHON, A.L./DIAMANTOPOULOS, A. (1997): Use and Non-Use of Export Information: Some Preliminary Insights Into Antecedents and Impact on Export Performance. *Journal of Marketing Management* 13. 135-151.

TAYLOR, R.S. (1991): Information Use Environments. *Progress in Communication Sciences* 10. 217-255.

TOOKEY, D. (1964): Factors Associated with Success in Exporting. *Journal of Management Studies* 20. N° 1. 48-66.

TUSHMAN, M./NADLER, N. (1978): Information Processing as an Integrating Concept in Organizational Design. *Academy of Management Review* 3. 613-624.

WEISS, C.H. (1977): *Using Social Research in Public Policy Making.* Lexington Books. D.C. Heath and Company.

WEISS, C.H. (1981): Measuring the Use of Evaluation. in: J. Ciarlo (ed.): *Utilizing Evaluation: Concepts and Measurement Techniques.* Beverley Hills, CA. Sage Publications Inc.

WEISS, C.H./BUCAVALAS, M.J. (1977): The Challenge of Social Research to Decision Making. in: C.H. Weiss (ed.) *Using Social Research in Public Policy Making.* Lexington Books. D. C. Heath and Company.

ZALTMAN, G./MOORMAN, C. (1988): The Importance of Personal Trust in the Use of Research. *Journal of Advertising Research* 28. N° 3. 16-24.

APPENDIX 1

Operationalisation of instrumental/conceptual use of export information

- Our confidence in making export decisions is increased as a result of information collected in this way.

- Decisions based on information collected in this way are more accurate than wholly intuitive ones.

- Without information gathered by this method, export decisions made would be very different.

- Our uncertainty associated with this export activity is greatly reduced by information acquired in this way.

- No export decision would be made without information collected by this method.

- The same piece of information collected in this way is often used for more than one decision.

- Information gathered by this method is preserved so that it can be used by individuals other than the person who collected it.

- The majority of the information gathered by this method is not used.

- Information collected in this way is translated into significant practical actions.

- Information is actively sought out from this method in response to a specific decision at hand.

- Information collected by this method is often used specifically to make a particular export decision.

- Information that is gathered in this way often has little decision relevance.

APPENDIX 2

Operationalisation of symbolic use of export information

- Information acquired in this way is sometimes manipulated in order to justify decisions really made on the basis of instinct.

- Key executives often distort information acquired by this method in passing it on.

- Information gathered by this method and used to justify an export decision is often collected and/or interpreted after the decision has been made.

- Information collected in this way is often used to back up hunches, prior to the implementation of an export decision.

- Information collected in this way frequently supports decisions made on other grounds.

- If information is difficult to obtain from this collection method, guesses are made instead.

- Information is often collected in this way to justify a decision already made.

- Information gathered in this way is often used to reinforce expectations.

- Information gathered in this way is often not considered in the making of decisions for which it was initially requested.

- Information is often gathered in this way merely to maintain good relationships with information suppliers.

- Information acquired in this way is sometimes taken into account to justify the cost of having acquired it.

APPENDIX 3

Export Performance Measures

Export Sales

(a)   *Export sales per employee* - defined as total export sales (in £) divided by the number of employees.

(b)   *Export sales per country* - defined as total export sales (in £) divided by the number of countries served.

Export Profitability

(c)   *Profitability of export sales in relation to domestic sales.* The question posed to the respondents was: *"Overall, how profitable are your export sales in relation to sales in the domestic market"* and was assessed on a five-point comparative rating scale ranging from 1 = "much less profitable" to 5 = "much more profitable".

Export Growth

(d)   *Growth or decline of export sales* - expressed as a percentage over the last three years.

(e)   *Growth or decline of export profits* - expressed as a percentage over the last three years.

Competitive Performance

(f)   *Competitive position* - the percentage of total export markets served in which the firm is (a) the market leader, (b) second to market leader, and (c) a major supplier.

(g)   *Performance in relation to competitors* - an index computed from the sum of four items measured on a seven-point scale. The question posed to the respondents was as follows: *"In relation to your major competitors, your export performance along the following items* (export sales, export profitability, export market share, rate of new market entry) *is..."*. The scale ranged from 1 = "much worse" to 7 = "much better".

Satisfaction with Export Operations

(h) *Level of satisfaction with export sales volume, export profitability, export market share and rate of new market entry*, an index computed from the sum of the above variables, each measured on a seven-point scale ranging from 1 = "very dissatisfied" to 7 = "very satisfied". The question was worded as follows: *"Overall, how satisfied are you with your performance along the following dimensions?"* The dimensions were as follows: export sales volume, export profitability, export market share, and rate of new market entry. The computed index was a simple sum of the scores on each item.

(i) *A weighted satisfaction score* - as above, but related to the importance of export objectives using Cavusgil and Zou's (1994) scheme. In order to calculate the weighted satisfaction score, the following algorithm was employed:

$$\frac{\left[\sum_{i=1}^{4} (Satisfaction_i \times Importance_i)\right] - 100}{6}$$

with $i = 1$ representing export sales volume,
          $i = 2$ representing export profitability,
          $i = 3$ representing export market share,
          $i = 4$ representing rate of new market entry.

Importance of export sales volume, profitability, market share and rate of new market entry was measured on a constant sum scale of 100 points, and the satisfaction ratings were measured on a seven-point scale, as already mentioned under (h) above. As a result, the multiplication of importance by the satisfaction ratings could result in values ranging from 100 to 700. The subtraction of 100 to the numerator, and the division by 6 were thus undertaken in order to obtain a weighted satisfaction score ranging from 0 to 100 (to enhance interpretability).

Overall Measure of Export Performance

(j) *A subjective measure of export performance* - a seven-point scale indicating overall perception of export performance, posed as follows: *"Overall, how would you rate your firm's export performance"* on a scale ranging from 1 = "poor" to 7 = "outstanding".

(k) *An index of overall performance* - derived by first standardising the measures described under (a)-(j) above and subsequently aggregating the standardised scores.

Giovanni Palmerio[*]

Information, Power, Efficiency: the Case of Small and Medium Size Italian Firms

---

[*]   I wish to thank Rita Carisano for the help she gave me in the writing of this essay.

1.   Introduction

The role of small and medium size firms in the development of modern industrial realities has for some time been the subject of growing attention by economists and economic policy authorities. This attention is not surprising if one considers that small firms, even though there are differences from country to country, constitute the supporting structure of the European Union's economy. In fact, 91% of European firms have fewer than 10 employees and only 0.1% of them have more than 499[1]. The European productive reality presents itself, therefore, as an economic space in which small firms face each other, in competition with each other and with a few large size firms.

Within this small firm scenario the Italian position appears particularly interesting: Italy is the country with the greatest number of firms (equal to about 3,920,000) and with a firm/inhabitant ratio second only to that of Greece.

To understand the factors of success, but also the elements of weakness that could compromise the vitality of this model of development, I will briefly review the steps through which small and medium size firms came to the fore in the European and Italian context and I will touch upon some characteristics of small and medium firms in Italy. Among these are the financing difficulties encountered by small firms, their innovative capacity and their contractual weakness both in the labor market and in other markets, of goods and productive factors.

2.   The European reality

A.   The general framework

The European productive reality, even with the evident differences that exist between the fifteen member countries, is substantially characterized by small firms.

---

[1]   The data contained in paragraphs 1 and 2 derive from computations carried out by Centro Studi Confindustria on Eurostat data for 1990.

In 1990, within the European Community (constituted by twelve countries) about 15.8 million firms existed. Adopting a classification by number of workers, which defines as small firms those with less than 100 workers and as medium size firms those with between 100 and 499 workers, one can affirm that 99.9% of firms were small and medium size. In 1990 there were 14.7 million firms with fewer than 10 employees, and only 13,000 firms employed more than 499 workers.

Together, small and medium size European firms, in the non primary sector, employed 68 million workers in 1990, which constituted 72% of the total employment in private firms.

With respect to the productive sectors to which these firms belong, we see that the most numerous are the firms that produce personal services (these represent 26.6% of the total), trading firms follow (22.3%), while manufacturing firms represent 11% of the total.

If we pass from aggregate data for the entire European Community to information about single member states we can see the size characteristics of firms in each national economy: Greece, Spain, Italy and Portugal present the smallest average firm size, respectively 3, 4, 4, 5 workers for each firm, which is lower than the average for the entire Community (6 workers). Germany, Luxembourg and Holland, instead, present the largest average firm size and higher than the European average. Germany, in particular among the European productive systems, is the one characterized by the greatest prevalence of large firms.

B.   The evolution of European manufacturing firms

The process of tendential decrease in average firm size, which characterizes industry in the principal European countries, began in the early seventies, and represented a noticeable inversion in tendency with respect to what had happened in the previous decades. In fact, while up until the years of the first oil shock the expansion in the industrial sector was accompanied by a growing productive concentration, in the following years a decline in the average firm size and a parallel increase in the share of employment in smaller firms was observed.

Beginning with the end of the second world war, in fact, and especially during the sixties, a firm's strategy for success emphasized economies of scale, i.e. the reduction of cost imputable to the increase in the quantity produced, and efficiency based on mass production and on the widening of the market to reach the optimal size.

The dimensions of firms and of the productive plants were progressively increased in this manner, while small firms had enormous difficulty in obtaining capital and new technologies. In the face of a demand for goods produced at low cost and of standard quality, small size constituted a handicap.

The double energy crisis of the seventies, removing from the general scenario the security of oil supplies at stable prices, altered the old equilibria. The response of firms was the abandonment of the strategy of verticalization prevailing in the previous decade and the adoption of productive decentralization.

The reversal had positive effects not only with respect to the readjustment of the costs of "decentralizing" firms, but also on the qualitative standards of the "decentralized" firms, who were able to acquire their own market niche, no longer based on imitative phenomena, but on autonomous innovative capacity.

Another factor of structural change which favored small size firms pertained to the increasing demand in the market for specialized products. This contributed to reducing the importance of large scale and, consequently, the minimization of costs: small firms are more flexible and adaptable than large and highly capital intensive firms and are able to respond to rapid changes in consumer preferences and to the continuous reduction in the life cycle of products.

During the eighties the process of restructuring and productive decentralizing continued.

Considering the four most advanced economies in the European Union - France, Germany, Italy and the United Kingdom -, between 1981 and 1991 the average firm size, expressed in number of employees, appears to have decreased in three of the four countries. The exception was Germany which was characterized by a higher average firm size, and this from the beginning of the observation period. The decrease appeared stronger for France and the United Kingdom, which began from much higher initial levels with respect to Italy.

The regularity with which the contraction in the average firm size is manifested suggests that even during the eighties the evolution of the European industrial structure was conditioned by systematic factors. The data pertaining to the share of workers for each size, in fact, describe a general tendency of employment to move toward small and medium size firms.

In conclusion, we can affirm that, except in Germany, in the main European countries, the relative number of small size firms appears to be constantly on the rise, and an increasing share of industrial employment is concentrated in these firms.

C.   A comparison with the United States and Japan

The European, American and Japanese entrepreneurial realities are, for historical and cultural reasons, very different, just as their patterns of development have been different. One proof of this difference is found in the different role that small firms have in each of the three areas. In Europe, as we have seen, small and medium size firms occupy a very important place, albeit with great differences at the national level, both from an economic and employment point of view as well as from the point of view of the social structure. The same cannot be said for the United States, where, instead, the role of small and medium size firms in the development process is very limited. Japan, on the other hand, based its own postwar development on small and very small firms and on their capacity to create employment.

Unfortunately, the quantitative aspects of the three realities can be compared on the basis of information pertaining to different periods, but not far apart (1988 for Europe and the United States and 1986 for Japan). The comparison indicates that, for the industrial sector alone, firms with fewer than 100 employees represent 90% of all firms in Europe, 87% in the United States and 89% in Japan.

With respect to employment shares in small firms classified by sector, in Italy 55.3% of employees in small firms are concentrated in manufacturing firms, in France 28.6%, in Germany 15.9%, in the United Kingdom 22%. Japan in this comparison is in second place after Italy, with 47% of those employed in small firms concentrated in manufacturing. The United States is, instead, much closer to the United Kingdom with 17.6%.

Another comparison pertains to average size, always to that of manufacturing firms. Japanese firms are the smallest with an average size of 70 employees; European firms with 76 employees follow. American firms are the largest on average with 137 employees.

3.   The Italian industrial structure: the role of small and medium size firms

The most recent data on the size structure of the Italian economy come from the last general census of the National Institute of Statistics (ISTAT) of 1991, from which it is possible to extract information both on firms in general and on manufacturing firms in particular.

It is important to underline that from this universe, firms with fewer than 10 employees are excluded; with respect to Eurostat data used for comparisons at the European level, therefore, this group of firms is much more limited, since firms with fewer than 10 employees are very numerous.

The 1991 census identified 235,920 firms in the entire economic sector, of which 66,465 have more than 19 employees. Taken together, these firms employ almost

8 million people, while more than 6 million are employed by firms with more than 19 employees. The average size of the Italian firm is 33.7 workers.

If we consider only the manufacturing sector, 90,622 firms were identified, with 3,799,888 workers: 38% of the total number of firms and 48% of total employment. 58% of the manufacturing firms are concentrated in the first size category (10-19 employees), which weighs in at almost 20% in terms of employment.

From the point of view of size, we can state that in Italy there are almost exclusively small and medium size firms: they are, in fact, 99.4%; the presence of the large firm is minimal, only 0.6%. In addition, within the same category of small and medium size firms, small size firms are preponderant: they represent 94.2% of the total.

In terms of employment, small and medium size firms create 73% of the jobs in the manufacturing sector.

To complete this analysis we must take some considerations of a sectoral nature into account. The manufacturing sectors in which small size firms prevail are those that are traditional for the Italian economy: textiles, apparel, and the mechanical, furniture and wood industries. In all these sectors, the average firm size is smaller than 500 employees. Large size, instead, prevails in the automobile sector, where firms with at least 500 employees are 10.5% of the large manufacturing firms.

With respect to location within the territory, Central Italy, in particular Tuscany and the Adriatic region, are the areas in which the prevalence of small firms is very strong. The provinces characterized by a larger relative presence of medium size firms cover, instead, a good part of the northern regions including Emilia. In Southern Italy, finally, large firms are present in very few centers, which are constituted by areas ofrecent industrialization.

The large firm characterizes, therefore, the oldest industrialization nuclei, that is the metropolitan areas of the so-called industrial triangle (Piedmont and Lombardy), and those southern areas in which the policies of "extraordinary intervention", which were undertaken from the beginning of the fifties, provided incentives for the settlement of large plants of basic industry. The diffusion of the medium size firm follows instead the borders of those areas in which the process of industrialization was consolidated in the sixties and seventies and is mainly the case in a large part of Veneto and Emilia.

4.   The recent evolution of Italian industry

In Italy the oil crisis of the seventies had stronger repercussions on the productive system than occurred in other industrialized countries. The causes of this are multiple.

To begin with, in Italy the crisis coincided with the conclusion of a particularly important historic period for the economy: that of the transformation from a predominantly agricultural country into an industrial country. This process occurred in the restricted twenty year period, from 1950 to 1970: the years of the "economic miracle".

In this period large firms played a strategic role; in any case, it was the small firm that bore the burden of the transformations, at least at the employment level, assuming both the role of social buffer, and economic.

The model of development based on small firms, therefore, seemed to be, especially in the fifties, the only possible way for the industrialization of Italy. And even when, in the sixties, big industry powerfully emerged, noticeably amplifying its employment base, it was still the small firm which contributed the most increment of employment in the Italian manufacturing industry.

At the beginning of the seventies, therefore, the national productive apparatus found itself in the very delicate phase of consolidation. Just at that moment, instead, almost in coincidence with the first oil crisis, a serious fracture came to modify the system of social relations that had previously regulated relationships in the labor market. The pressures exercised by growing unionization led to one of the presuppositions that of the availability of the labor force at low and substantially stable costs on which the take-off of the Italian economy had been based be no longer valid.

On top of these domestic factors, which however would trigger structural updating processes, was added the element of the energy crisis which was an external shock.

Previously the solution adopted by industrialized countries, and first by the United States, consisted in counterbalancing the repeated increases in the price of oil through inflation and the devaluation of the dollar, the base currency for the regulation of international payments. At the same time it was attempted, with little luck in truth, to put into place policies of energy savings and diversification of the sources of energy. However, the dependence on oil had by then reached such a high level (it represented about 80% of total energy consumption) that it did not allow for the use of alternative energy sources in the short term.

At the structural level, those most hit by the crisis were large firms; at the sectoral level, those operating in the areas of strongly energy-oriented activity, among these, in particular, steel, ship-building and partly textiles.

Also in Italy, the response of firms was the beginning of a process of deverticalization and productive decentralization, continued in the course of the eighties.

To analyze the evolution of firms in Italy in the years 1971-1991 the most complete sources of information are those derived by censi, carried out by the National Institute of Statistics (ISTAT) every ten years (1971, 1981, 1991) on the entire industrial sector.

The tendency toward an increase in the share of small size firms and in the share of workers employed by them occurred in both census intervals. For the entire manufacturing sector, if firms with fewer than 10 employees are excluded, one can state that there was a decrease in the number offirms, an overall fall in employment and, at the same time, a reduction in the average size of firms measured in terms of number of employees.

This information furnishes a clear enough picture of the fundamental characteristics of the evolution of the Italian industrial structure in there cent past. The re-emergence, in the seventies, of small size firms as creators of new businesses and employment seemed to be offset, in the succeeding decade, by a stop of the expansion of the productive base. Smaller size firms- at least those with more than 10 employees- maintained greater dynamism, but in a context in which the overall level of employment fell not only with respect to the 1981 level, but also to that of 1971.

From 1981 to 1991 the share of employees in firms with more than 499 workers fell by 19.6%, the share for firms with fewer than 100 increased by 17.8%.

This dynamic is independent of any sectoral composition effect. At the disaggregated level the role that small firms play in terms of contribution to employment is, in fact, substantially uniform.

5. The economic performance of small and medium size Italian firms

To reach an evaluation of the performance of small and medium size Italian firms, we can refer only to some large sample studies. The censi, in fact, consider only the number and size of the firms.

The available data are those relative to an analysis of manufacturing firms carried out by the Observatory of Mediocredito Centrale on a sample of 4,431 firms with more than 10 employees in the period 1992-1994[2].

A first important aspect pertains to the propensity of small and medium size firms to export. If firms with more than 10 employees are considered together with reference to 1994, we note that the export/sales ratio tends to grow constantly with size, but it decreases in the highest class (over 500 employees).

Medium size firms - between 51 and 500 employees - appear to be the most open to foreign markets with a percentage between 39.2% and 40% of sales abroad. These firms belong mainly to specialized mechanical industry sectors and to traditional sectors such as textiles, apparel, leather, shoes and wood.

Other very important aspects of firm performance pertain to sales, value added, cost of labor.

In 1994 the class that presented the highest value added per employee was that with more than 500 employees. The smallest class - 11-20 employees - was also the one with the smallest value of this ratio.

Considering a very meaningful index of economic structure, the ratio between value added and sales, we can state that in the smallest firm class, that with 11-20 employees, this ratio is equal to 21.5% and in the largest class (more than 500 workers) to 25.9%. The class that shows the largest value in the ratio (27.8%) is the one that includes firms with 21-50 employees.

With respect to the ratio between cost of labor and value added, then, it grows as size increases: it is, in fact, equal to 58.3% for the class of 11-20 employees and equal to almost 60.9% for the class of more than 500 employees.

If the traditional economic-financial ratios are analyzed, two interesting data are found, which confirm the vitality of small size firms. The return on invested

---

2   Mediocredito Centrale, "Indagine sulle imprese manifatturiere", sixth report on Italian industry and on industrial policy, Rome 1997.

capital (measured with the ROI ratio, which is given by the ratio between gross income excluding financing expenses and the capital invested in a given year) assumes the highest values for the classes of 11-20 employees and 21-50 employees (respectively 7% and 7.9%); then it assumes decreasing values as size increases. A noticeable fall appears,instead, in the return on capital invested in large size firms: it reaches 5.6% in those with more than 500 employees.

Analysis of ROE, that is the return on equity (which is given by the ratio between the firm's income and owners' equity gross of reserves), confirms the vitality of small size firms, in spite of the existence, for these firms, of a big structural problem due to high debt and the cost of servicing it.

A last important reflection that should be made and that will be the subject of later explanation pertains to the financial structure of Italian firms and in particular small and medium ones. Italian firms present an unbalanced structure, because they have excessive indebtedness and, in this context, have excessive short term debts. The cost of this indebtedness, furthermore, is higher for small than for large firms. With respect, finally, to the duration of the debts, the classes of firms, all of them, characterized by small and medium sizes present an incidence of short term financial indebtedness over total financial indebtedness greater than 70%, which reaches 76% for the class with between 21 and 50 employees. Vice versa, the class with more than 500 employees shows a value of this incidence equal to about 57%.

6. Size structure in relation to ownership structure of Italian firms

The analysis of the size structure of the productive system must be evaluated also in relation to the ownership structure of firms.

On this point some recent studies of the Bank of Italy have made information available both on the concentration of ownership and on the means of control of firms[3]. In particular, one study conducted on a sample of 1,000 industrial firms with at least 50 workers in 1993 permits us to estimate the distribution of the ownership shares for all manufacturing firms.

The ownership of these firms is very concentrated (the average of the largest ownership share is equal to 66.3%) and the concentration grows with the firm's size. Passing from the small to the large firm, the number of cases in which the largest share coincides with the entire capital grows.

This result is an antithesis with respect to what we might expect and what actually occurs in other countries, that is a greater separation between ownership and control as the size of the firm grows. In Italy, instead, due to the strong diffusion of hierarchical groups, in the class of firms of large size there is more frequent presence of firms belonging to groups, in which the largest share is represented by the participation of control retained by the holding.

With respect to the type of capital participants, the available information allows us to estimate that natural persons possess 48% overall of the capital of firms with at least 50 employees. Considering only medium-small firms, the available information indicates that the presence of the founders of the firm or their descendents among the owners is very common. This constitutes a further confirmation of the importance of the direct and family ownership in medium-small firms.

The analyses carried out by the Bank of Italy allow, furthermore, the verification of the characteristics of the "models of control" prevalent in Italian firms. 87% of Italian industrial firms with at least 50 employees are controlled through the possession of a majority of the ownership shares. Differently from what occurs in other countries, the phenomenon assumes particular importance in large size firms. This result derives from the extraordinary diffusion in Italy of the model of control based on the pyramid group. By pyramid group is meant a group of

---

3   Banca d'Italia, "Il mercato della proprietà e del controllo delle imprese: aspetti teorici e istituzionali", Rome 1994.

firms, each endowed with an autonomous legal personality and controlled directly or indirectly by a single owner (a person or a family). This model, in addition to offering solutions to problems of internal organization, offers the controlling entrepreneur the possibility of expanding control without contributing more of his own capital.

From the data the existence of a large number of firms with at least 50 workers organized in the group form (55.4%) emerges. The diffusion of the phenomenon grows as the size of the firm increases.

7.   The difficulties that small and medium firms encounter in financing their operations

The difficulties of access to credit for smaller size firms represent a characteristic rather common in the European Union financial systems. In Italy, however, the obstacles to the financing of small firms assume particular relevance for reasons that have to do first of all with the greater weight that small firms have with respect to what occurs in other countries of the European Union and in the second place, to the peculiarity of the Italian financial system.

In recent years an abundant amount of literature has developed on the tie between the economy's financing structure and growth, which shows how removing savings of firms, orienting them toward nonproductive uses (above all current public spending), has strong negative effects on the real economy. It has also been shown that the presence of financial intermediaries is advantageous, to the extent they insure better management of liquidity and better diversify savers' risk, stimulating long term economic growth.

These analyses induce reflection on a structural problem of the Italian financial system: the heavy burden of public debt on the financial market and on family savings, which reduces the resources allocated to production and rigidifies interest rates, which fall only with difficulty.

Then there is the problem of the marginal role that risk capital and the stock exchange play in the Italian financial system and conversely, the almost exclusive role of banks in the external financing of firms.

These distortions of the Italian financial system are reflected, amplified, in smaller size firms, which have not developed a true financing function internally, as large firms have done, but have often been restricted to self financing, and therefore to the results of industrial management.

The financing model of Italian firms has three principal characteristics: it is strongly dependent on indebtedness to banks; it is skewed toward short term indebtedness; both of these circumstances assume a growing weight as one passes from large size firms to small ones.

If one looks at the composition of the sources of external financing needs, several differences between smaller and larger size firms emerge. For the smaller firms, the importance of risk capital appears secondary, while resort to bank indebtedness is very high; in larger firms, it is the reverse: the role of risk capital grows and the presence of indebtedness declines. In addition, the larger external exposure of small firms is accompanied by an increase in short term indebtedness.

The comparison with other European countries underlines the anomaly of the Italian case. In this comparison, in fact, the relationship between short term and long term bank debts is exactly the opposite for Italian firms. In Italy, on average, about 70% of bank indebtedness of firms is short term. French and German firms, on the contrary, mainly resort (68% and 78% respectively) to long term credit[4]. Furthermore, in Italy, the burden of short term bank debts over total debts assumes, large importance for small firms.

In general there seems to exist a close correlation between the increase in indebtedness and its composition by maturity. As the firm's degree of indebted-

---

[4]   Data of Centro Studi Confindustria.

ness increases, banks tend to prefer renegotiable short term loans; the increase in indebedness signals, in fact, a greater degree of risk for the bank.

The presence of a large share of debt, and, of this, the high share of short term debt, has significant consequences for small firms from three different aspects: the availability of credit, its cost and risk.

With respect to the availability of credit, medium and long term loans have always represented a minor component of the overall financing of small firms. Recently, furthermore, their volume appears not only small but also in noticeable decline. The contraction of medium and long term credit allocated to small and medium firms is attributable to the reduction in subsidized credit in recent years and to the reduction in that financing allocated by development policies for the support of small firms. For the entire economy the incidence of subsidized credit out of total long term financing passed from 25.5% in 1990 to 13.7% in 1996. What was reduced was essentially the subsidized credit to industry and in particular loans granted on the basis of laws providing incentive to small and medium firms. In fact, for these firms, the ratio between subsidized credit and total long term financing in 1996 was equal to 2.2%[5].

But the difficulty of small firms in obtaining funds depends also on the fact that to the progressive decline in medium and long term credit - and,as a part of it, subsidized credit - was added, in recent years, the strong slowing of short term bank loans. In 1992 total bank loans increased by 11.6%; in 1993 the rate of growth was equal to 4%; in 1994 and in 1995 it was equal to 1.1% and 3.2% respectively, and in 1996 to 1.7%[6].

A sample investigation conducted by the Bank of Italy[7] has shown that in 1993 about 50% of firms spent at least 5% less than that planned for investment, and this occurred mainly because of the unavailability of external financing. In three

---

[5]   Data of the Bank of Italy.
[6]   Banca d'Italia "Relazione Annuale per il 1996", Rome 1997.
[7]   Banca d'Italia "Indagine sugli investimenti e sull'occupazione nella trasformazione industriale", Rome 1994.

years, 1990-1993, there was almost a quadrupling of the share of firms that experienced credit "rationing", that is those firms that were willing to go into debt at the prevailing market interest rate, but did not obtain the requested financing.

With respect to the cost of external financing, from data of the Centrale dei Bilanci[8] we see that for smaller firms the incidence of financing costs on the operating margin is increasing; after having decreased to the smallest level of 36% in 1983, the ratio rose again to 49% in 1991 and showed a small decrease in the following two years.

The reasons why the cost of indebtedness is higher for smaller firms are due to several factors. A first reason is due to the absence of sources of financing other than bank indebtedness and to the difficulty of accessing those few means available. Small firms not listed on the stock exchange cannot, for example, by Italian legislation, issue savings shares. Until the end of 1994, furthermore, interest on bonds issued by unlisted firms was taxed at a rate of 30%, against 12.5% for listed firms.

A second reason that contributes to increasing the cost of money for small firms is represented by the segmentation of the credit market, which often leads to a high dependency of the debtor firm on the bank that finances it. The credit market appears, in fact, segmented in local markets in which small banks with substantial market power operate, so that, to a large extent, the negotiations with their clientele in granting credit can often give rise to differential treatment. The localization of the bank itself is, in this regard, an important element: a large part of the banking system is constituted by institutes - mainly Casse di Risparmio and Banche Popolari - whose size seems irrelevant with respect to the national market, but is decisive with respect to the local market in which the bank operates.

---

[8]   Centrale dei Bilanci, "Economia e finanza delle imprese italiane", Bancaria Editrice, Rome 1995.

A typical phenomenon of the Italian banking system is, furthermore, the fragmentation of overall financing of individual firms among several banks.

Each firm has on average 2.6 financing banks, and their number grows as the size of the firm increases. For smaller firms, which receive loans not greater than 1 billion liras, only one bank participates in the financing. About 33 institutions participate in the financing of firms with credit of 500 billion and more; 50% of credit granted is concentrated on average in 5.5 banks, but to cover the second half of the financing almost 28 banks are required, while financing of the leading bank does not exceed 20% of the total[9].

An international comparison may help to show the higher cost of money for Italian firms with respect to their competitors. Italy has the highest interest rate on bank loans, in nominal terms as well as in real terms, in particular with respect to checking account operations. The interest rate for smaller firms is around 14.2%, while it is equal to 9.3% in France and 11.5% in Germany[10].

Contributing, finally, to the riskiness of credit to small and medium firms, are factors of instability, connected to non substitutability of debt as a source of financing for small firms, as well as the variability of interest rates on debt, which is transmitted, amplified, to the profitability of the firms.

In conclusion we may state that the imbalances in the financial structure of firms, mainly small firms, originate from several causes. Briefly we may identify three principal aspects.

A first aspect is related to the weakness of the Italian financial system which is characterized even today by a very limited supply of financial instruments: it is enough to think that 73% of the Italian financial market is constituted by government bonds.

---

[9]   Computations of the Centro Studi Confindustria on data of the Bank of Italy for 1993.
[10]   Computations of the Centro Studi Confindustria on data of the Bank of Italy for 1995.

A second aspect is related to the fact that the tax system favors financing in the form of debt.

A third aspect is inherent in the lack of flexibility of firm ownership models and to the mainly family character of private firms. Differently from other industrialized countries, in Italy financial markets and management play a modest role. The choice of maintaining control of the firm and excluding shareholders outside the family circle would impede the search for external risk capital even if the market permitted it. In this respect the necessity of also developing risk capital markets for small firms is becoming pressing.

In this regard, a project for a second stock market in which securities of solid and profitable firms but of medium-small size, may be quoted and exchanged, with strict admission requirements but not as limiting as those of the first market, deserves comment. In particular corporations and limited liability partnerships and cooperatives whose ownership is represented by shares could be listed. The firm assets should be sufficient to guarantee a certain volume of exchange; the most recent balance sheet should show a profit and ordinary management should show positive results. The firms should have been in business for at least five years and have obtained audited financial statements. The advantage of this market would be mainly in the costs of admission, which constitute in general a strong deterrent for firms to become listed and that would be, in the second market, completely accessible.

8.   The innovative ability of small firms

Among the factors that for some time led many economists to maintain that there is a different behavior between small and large firms is certainly the conviction that small and medium firms encounter difficulty in assimilating technical progress. Recently, however, the innovative ability of small firms has been reevaluated, so much so that it is maintained that, at least in some sectors, small firms constitute the engine of technological change and are surpassing the innovative performances of large firms.

The role of small and medium firms in innovation and in the diffusion of technology is larger than the official data suggest. In fact, annual expenditures for research and development (R&D) do not represent a sufficiently reliable indicator of the innovative potential of a firm, since there is no clear connection between the expenditure for R&D and the stock of knowledge accumulated over time, as this does not derive exclusively from the research activity.

As the quantification of R&D depends on the presence of centers that have well defined costs (laboratories), research activity appears mainly in medium-large firms. In small and medium firms, instead, the commitment to research, when it is present, appears to be rather modest, since the small size limits the ability to dedicate resources to aims too removed from the immediate needs of the market.

The role of small and medium firms appears to be larger when other indicators are considered, such as the adoption of new technologies of production, the patents applied for or the statistics on new products and processes actually introduced into the markets.

According to a study of ISTAT[11], which gathered information on a sample of more than 35,000 firms, there are 12,900 innovative firms in Italy with a number of employees between 20 and 99: these firms constitute more than 77% of the firms that have declared they have introduced some form of innovation. Of these firms, only 12.9% introduced complex innovations, whether product, process or organizational; this percentage increases to about 21% for firms with a number of workers between 100 and 499 and reaches 29% for firms with at least 500 employees.

Considering at the same time the sector to which the firm belongs and its size, it is possible to state that small innovative firms are concentrated in the machine working sector. Within the traditional sectors medium size firms show better innovative ability, with the highest values in the wood and furniture sector and in staple food products.

---

[11]   ISTAT, "Investigation into the Diffusion of Technological Innovation in Italian Manufacturing Industry", Rome 1993.

With respect to the type of innovation, the ISTAT study shows that small firms tend mainly to introduce process innovations rather than product innovations, especially in the traditional sectors; in sectors of high technological intensity, complex innovation becomes important also for small firms. Larger firms are more oriented toward product innovation than are smaller firms, although the larger differences between process and product innovations are due more to the sector to which the firm belongs than to size. Only 21.3% of the firms with fewer than 100 employees carry out formalized R&D activity, while that percentage rises to 75% for the local units with at least 500 employees.

The other investigation, conducted by Mediocredito Centrale[12] on a sample of 4,431 firms, confirms (with respect to 1994) a marked attitude to innovation of small and medium firms, reporting at the same time a larger amount of innovations introduced overall. 51.3% of the firms with up to 20 employees included in the sample and 67.2% of firms with a number of employees between 21 and 500 introduced innovations between 1992 and 1994. The percentage of small innovative firms has increased according to this study, in specialized sectors and in high technology sectors. In the high technology sectors with large economies of scale, such as pharmaceuticals, electronics and chemicals, the role played by large firms is decisive. The respective roles of large and small firms is more balanced in specialized sectors, while a certain innovative advantage for small firms is reported in traditional sectors.

Interesting considerations may be made on the sources of acquisition of knowledge on the part of firms: they may be divided into internal and external.

Among the internal sources, learning in the course of the production process represents the principal channel of acquisition of knowledge necessary for the innovative activity of small firms, i.e. those with up to 50 employees; in the next size class, 51-200 employees, the importance of knowledge acquired in research laboratories increases instead.

---

[12]   Mediocredito Centrale, op. cit.

Among the external sources, small firms use mainly scientific and technical publications, together with the advice of experts and research companies. The importance of collaboration activity with the university world is marginal and less than average. This fact is consistent with the hypothesis that small firms commit themselves mainly to development and adaptation of scientific and technical knowledge already acquired in their own sector, rather than to the introduction of radical innovations. The small collaboration with universities puts in evidence the need to create public and private institutions to act as intermediaries between university research and firms for the purpose of the diffusion of technological innovation.

9.   The public instruments of research support

In Italy the problem of transferring technology to small firms has not received the same attention from public authorities as in other countries. Law number 46 of 1982 is the most important rule for the support of research and innovation. Article 3 therein provides such support to small and medium firms, but this article was never made operational.

On the basis of the research previously cited from Mediocredito Centrale, the firms that benefitted from financial incentives during the period 1992-1994 were equal to 21.2% of firms with up to 20 employees included in the sample and 32.8% of those with a number of employees between 21 and 50. For firms with more than 50 employees, percentages greater than 50% are recorded. The main obstacle to the utilization of funds on the part of small firms is the high bureaucratization of the financing procedure, which requires on average three years of time between the date of submission of the request and the eventual granting of the financing.

Instead a greater contribution to the innovative activity of small firms was furnished by the special rotating fund for technological innovation (FIT), instituted by the Ministry of the Interior with the objective of supporting investment programs aimed at the introduction of technological innovation. In the period 1983-1992, 28.9% of the total investments by the fund went to small and medium firms, with a concentration of the assistance mainly in the machine-working, chemical and food sectors.

The service centers for technological transfer are particularly relevant for the development of the innovative abilities of small firms. These centers, which operate mainly at the local level, are often promoted jointly by public entities (mainly Regions) and private agents. However, the experiences of scientific and technological parks are still rare; on the basis of the experience of other industrialized countries, these institutions could favor the birth of small and medium size firms and could represent an important channel for the diffusion of technological innovations.

In conclusion, the picture that emerges from the different studies we have considered is that of a limited innovative attitude of small industrial firms in Italy, both compared to the large national firms, and compared to the small firms of other industrialized countries. There exists in fact a limited number of small firms operating on the technological frontier,which get their origin and their source of growth from significant innovation, which can often be patented. In contrast, we have a large number of small firms, that operate in more or less mature sectors, characterized by limited technological opportunities and imitative innovations.

10. The labor market and small and medium size firms

Different empirical studies have emphasized how the share of employment in small firms over the total has increased in the last decade. This fact, which brings into evidence the role of small firms in the creation of jobs, can be observed not only in Italy, but also in all the main industrialized countries: in 1990 72% of employment in the non-primary sector in the European Union could be attributed to small and medium size firms[13].

---

[13] Computations of the Centro Studi Confindustria on Eurostat data.

In Italy today small and medium size firms represent 73% of the employment in the manufacturing sector, and during the ten years between 1981 and 1991 they increased their contribution to employment by 7 percentage points, buffering the effect of the exit of workers from larger size firms which occurred in the same period.

In particular, many studies have shown that:
– independent of the employment balance, the gross flow of job creation and destruction are much larger in small firms and, in general, they decrease as the firm's dimension increases;
– the separation rates (i.e. the gross movement flow of workers, both keeping the available jobs constant, and because of new hiring and lay-offs) are also higher, the smaller the firm's dimension;
– the share of young people in total employment decreases as the size of the firm increases, so that the younger workers are concentrated in small firms;
– in small firms not only the share of young people in the entrance flow is very large, but also in the exit flow from employment.

This information allows us to outline the role of the small firm in the labor market.

The greater turnover of workers in the small firm is due to the smaller possibility of filling vacancies with workers that hold other positions inside the firm, so that more people are hired in the external market. From the point of view of workers, this means fewer career opportunities inside small firms and therefore the quest for improvement through the transfer to other firms. Many of these workers are young people who, after the first working experience in small firms, leave them in preference for larger firms, characterized by larger opportunities for internal mobility and a greater legal protection of jobs.

It follows that small and medium size firms have a very important role from the point of view of increasing employment, since they tend to hire, on average, younger and less qualified personnel than larger firms and to provide on-the-job training which tends to compensate for the chronic deficiencies of the Italian technical and professional training system. This helps to explain the fact that in small firms pay levels are on average lower and the need, for those firms, to resort to the external market to fill positions that require high specialization and professional experience.

With respect to the regulatory framework, this is not favorable to the small firm, not because of rules specifically addressed to it, but rather due to the general characteristics of the regulation of the job market, which make it basically rigid and not very sensitive to the business cycle.

For this reason it is opportune to describe - along essential lines - the structure of the job market in Italy and to see, then, how the size of the firm is used as a discriminating factor in the application of the rules.

11. The regulation of the job market in Italy

A brief summary of Italian law may be made through the following basic points:
- there is a "typical work relationship"; relationships that have "atypical" characteristics are permitted only as exceptions, in cases defined by law;
- the atypical solutions must be previously authorized by organs of the State;
- through collective bargaining the social parties may define derogations, in limited cases, of the typical situation;
- through the agreement between the parties the procedures can be facilitated and can become less costly;
- in the case of ascertained irregularity, the typical situation is reestablished.

This system, made confusing by a quarter of a century of legislative production and union practices, in fact impedes the development of all those forms of flexibility in work that would permit an increase in employment. The lack of functional flexibility (i.e. of the possibility of employing a worker in different positions), of numeric flexibility (i.e. the possibility of hiring and laying off according to need) and of the possibility to enter into contracts with adequate trial periods, which allow patterns of entrance salaries (lower than the salary received by employed workers) or regimes of differentiated hours, in fact, make the demand for labor on the part of firms basically rigid.

Furthermore, beyond the limitation in the type of contract, there are real obstacles to the free choice of workers you are going to hire, such as: the obligation to use the (public) office of employment; the obligation to hire a quota of handicapped or persons belonging to socially protected categories; the obligation to reserve a share of new jobs for the weak part of the market (unemployed for more than two years, persons on a mobility list, etc.).

Moreover, if the legislation is rigid in the case of hiring, it is not less rigid in the case of lay-offs. In the case of individual lay-offs, the contract can be dissolved only for good cause or for a justified reason. In firms that employ up to 15 employees a lay-off that does not meet these criteria is punishable by the rehiring of the worker or by compensation for damages which go from a minimum of 2.5 months' pay to a maximum of 14. If the firm has more than 15 employees, the cost of a lay-off adjudged impermissible is at least 5 months' pay in addition to reintegration into the work place.

Collective lay-offs have legal foundation in a State law. The law establishes that firms with more than 15 employees may proceed to collective lay-offs (that is of at least 5 persons) in the case of cessation, reduction or transfer to other activities. The firm must initiate a procedure of negotiation with the unions to discuss the reasons for the reduction in personnel, with reference to its extent and to the characteristics of the employees to lay off. The employees laid off with this procedure are registered on unemployment lists (the so called mobility lists), which give them the right to special treatment, including the payment of an indemnity, which, however, is very low.

With respect to wages, the law imposes minimum wages and tends to compress the differences in salaries among sectors, among qualifications, among regions.

The rigidity of the wage structure has effects in several directions: it reduces mobility and above all favors the less qualifiedworkers.

Until July of 1992 there was in Italy the "indennità di contingenza", also called "scala mobile", which in the preceeding seventeen years had had an important role both on the wage dynamics and on the size of wage differentials. The mechanism of the "scala mobile", in fact, consisted of updating wages, rapidly, with the increase in prices. The "scala mobile", however, not only represented a vicious circle of transmission of inflationary tensions, but also had direct effects on wage differentials, by reducing them. In 1992 this mechanism of indexation was eliminated.

A final comment about the protection of workers and the unemployed. In the course of the seventies the difficult situation after the first oil shock gave rise to a profound modification of the instruments, until then in reality very limited, that legislation made available in case of business crises with consequences on employment. These modifications conformed to the principle of defending the work place as opposed to laying off: collective lay-offs were not regulated by law until 1991, while there was great resort to social buffers, in particular to the wage supplementation fund, called "cassa integrazione guadagni" (CIG). The use of this instrument, originally conceived as a form of income support for workers in case of temporary reduction in hours worked, was extended to situations of business restructuring and sectoral crises.

In 1991 a law rationalized the criteria for using this instrument and limited the maximum duration of enjoyment of the "cassa integrazione"; moreover it also regulated the area of collective lay-offs and introduced the mobility lists. These lists, in which workers who lost their jobs following a collective lay-off are registered, provide support, even if limited, to the worker's income; furthermore, firms are encouraged to hire workers on the lists through special incentives.

Another instrument, introduced in 1993, which helps firms to reduce laying-off personel is that of solidarity contracts. These consist of an agreement, at the firm level, to reduce the hours of work with the State intervening in the form of income support for workers, for a maximum of two years.

12. Size as a discriminant for some provisions of the law

Among the legal provisions that regulate the job market some provide exceptions for small firms: there is a special regulation for artisan firm[14], but mainly a differentiation on the basis of size is provided. Typically this differentiation consists in imposing a threshold - in terms of number of workers - below which laws otherwise valid for all other firms do not apply.

Overall, the distinction between firms of up to 15 employees and those of larger size prevails, present even in the statute of workers (Statuto dei lavoratori)[15]; for trading firms the threshold is considered 50 employees. The main differences connected to the threshold of 15 workers pertain to the hiring, lay-offs, CIG and solidarity contracts: workers of larger firms are more protected from the risk of losing their jobs and the resulting income.

This characteristic, together with the accessibility to prolonged income support in case of employment crises (extraordinary wage supplementation fund, i.e. "cassa integrazione guadagni straordinaria", mobility list), a support mainly enjoyed by workers of larger firms, reduces the supply of specialized workers needed by small firms. It should be remembered, then, that smaller firms may be penalized with respect to social buffers, especially when the available funds are limited, as in the case of solidarity contracts: the serious social problems

---

[14] The framework law for the artisan firms, issued on August 8, 1985, defines as artisan the firm that is personally carried on by an entrepreneur that carries out mainly his own work, even manual, in the productive process. The artisan firm must not, moreover, surpass a maximum number of employees, which is different depending on the type of activity carried on. In particular these size limits differ according to whether or not there is serial production or whether the firm operates in the sector of traditional artistic works and clothing made to measure, in the transport sector or in that of building construction.

[15] This is a law issued on July 20, 1970.

connected to the crises of the largest firms, in fact, generally arouse greater interest of the union organizations and of the government.

With reference to hiring, firms with more than 10 employees must reserve 12% of new hiring for the long term unemployed, workers on the mobility list or otherwise belonging to the "weak parts" of the job market, while for firms that have more than 35 workers there is the obligation to reserve 15% of the total jobs for the handicapped and other protected categories.

With respect to individual lay-offs, as we have seen, the law provides, in case of illegitimate lay-off, monetary sanctions even for the smallest productive units, but the sanctions are heavier for firms that have more than 15 employees. Collective lay-offs are regulated beyond the threshold of 15 employees, with further distinction between industrial and trading firms.

On the social buffer side, the resort to the ordinary wage supplementation fund (cassa integrazione guadagni ordinaria) does not have inferior size limits, but law number 236 of 1993 and later decrees have extended the time limits of using this fund for firms between 5 and 50 employees. The "cassa integrazione guadagni straordinaria" is reserved for firms with more than 15 employees (more than 50 in trading firms). The access to the mobility list, which originally applied only to collective lay-offs, has been extended by law number 236 of 1993 to workers individually laid-off by firms of up to 15 employees for reasons of reduction, transformation or cessation of business. In solidarity contracts, the intervention of the State guarantees less coverage of wages and fewer incentives to firms which are outside the field of application of CIG, that is essentially small firms.

There is another important aspect that characterizes the small firm in relation to the job market: this pertains to the serious insufficiency of public intervention in the field of professional formation, which causes greater costs of search, selection and training of workers for all firms, but in particular for small firms, which face higher employee turnover rates and absorb a high share of young people in their first jobs.

Giovanni PALMERIO

Résumé

Information, pouvoir, efficience : le cas des petites et moyennes entreprises italiennes

Les petites et moyennes entreprises suscitent à l'heure actuelle un intérêt croissant tant au niveau de la recherche que de la part des pouvoirs publics. Elles relèvent en effet de modes de fonctionnement particuliers qui s'avèrent efficients au niveau micro économique (capacité d'adaptation, créativité, résultats) et macro économique (contribution au développement économique et à l'emploi).

Le cas de l'Italie est particulièrement instructif en raison de l'ampleur du phénomène. Au regard des trois concepts affichés dans le titre du chapitre ce sont les facteurs de succès mais aussi les faiblesses stratégiques qui sont étudiées ici. Dans le processus de création de valeur, l'incidence de l'information sur les modalités de financement, ainsi que la création et la transmission du savoir est analysée.

Zusammenfassung

Information, Macht, Effizienz : die italienischen Klein- und Mittelbetriebe

Die kleinen und mittleren Unternehmen sind derzeit Gegenstand wachsenden Interesses sowohl in der Forschung als auch seitens der öffentlichen Hand. Sie weisen in der Tat besondere Funktionsformen auf, die ihre Effizienz sowohl in betriebswirtschaftlicher Hinsicht (Anpassungsfähigkeit, Kreativität, Ergebnisse) wie auch volkswirtschaftlich (durch ihren Beitrag zur Entwicklung der Gesamtwirtschaft wie auch des Arbeitsmarktes) unter Beweis stellen.

Was diesbezüglich in Italien geschieht, ist wegen des Umfangs des Phänomens besonders lehrreich. Im Hinblick auf die drei, im Titel des Beitrages angekündigten Begriffe werden hier Erfolgsfaktoren wie auch Strategieschwächen untersucht. Gegenstand der Analyse ist die Frage, wie sich Information auf die Finanzierungsmodalitäten und auf die Schaffung und Weitergabe von Wissen im Wertschöpfungsprozeß auswirken.

Constantinos C. Markides
and Elizabeth A.M. Tracy

The Valuation Consequences of International Joint Ventures: A Learning Perspective

"In retrospect, the emergence and proliferation of alliances, dating from about 1970, may turn out to be as significant an organizational innovation as the moving assembly line and the multi-divisional structure."[1]

1. Introduction

In recent years, there has been a growing emphasis on the use of alternative organizational forms such as joint ventures and strategic alliances to deal with the competitive pressures and challenges presented by today's business environment. Particularly in the international arena, co-operative ventures have become increasingly popular. For example, a McKinsey analysis of U.S. firms that have joint ventures with one or more foreign partners shows a six-fold increase in the number of new ventures established annually from 1976 to 1987 (Hladik and Linden, 1989). Data collected at INSEAD on cooperative ventures formed between 1979 and 1993 show a similar rate of increase in new partnerships world-wide (see figure 1).

Especially within Europe, cooperative ventures have become wide-spread. Ventures between European partners account for nearly a quarter of those tracked in the INSEAD study, and ventures involving at least one European partner account for approximately two thirds. Also, both the McKinsey and the INSEAD studies show European partners are the clear favourite for U.S. firms.

Enthusiasm for cooperative ventures in Europe can be explained by several factors; in addition to general world-wide trends, we see:
– The 1992 program of economic integration compelling European firms to cooperate across borders in order to achieve economies of scale and greater competitiveness.
– Non-European firms seeking access to the large single market.

---

[1]   Teece, David J. (1992), Competition, Cooperation and Innovation: Organizational Arrangements for Regimes of Rapid Technological Progress", *Journal of Economic Behaviour and Organization*, 18, pp. 1-25.

- Firms striving for a toe-hold in developing economies in Central and Eastern Europe, as well as Southern Europe.
- Privatization of state-owned companies throughout Europe leading to several cooperative ventures.

Figure 1: New partnerships by year

Thus both European and non-European firms seeking opportunities in Europe have raced into markets to secure positions with a limited number of potential partners.

While they may be newly popular, joint ventures are hardly a new phenomenon. In their early study Stopford and Wells (1972) examined the manufacturing subsidiaries of 187 firms in the year 1966. They found that more than one third of these firms had joint venture partners in at least 40 percent of their foreign manufacturing operations, and fewer than 18 percent had no foreign joint ventures at all. Joint ventures have long been used as a means of extracting raw materials, or to enter new markets with existing products. In fact, joint ventures were frequently the only means of entry into certain countries (Contractor, 1990).

As Porter and Fuller (1986) point out, these "tactical" joint ventures used to access markets or raw materials are still common. However many of the modern day joint ventures have become more "strategic" in nature. Indeed, in her study Hladik (1985) found that while U.S. foreign joint ventures formed prior to 1975 did not encompass much beyond the manufacture of existing products and sales to the local market, a large percentage of those formed after 1975 involved the development, manufacturing and marketing of new products. In addition, she found that by the 1980's, almost half of all new international joint ventures exported to other foreign markets. In another study, Hladik and Linden (1989) note that joint ventures seem to be moving from the end of the business chain (in sales and Marketing), back toward the beginning of the business chain. For example, the joint ventures in their sample which had an R&D component more than tripled from 1976 to 1987.

Our study also finds a trend towards more "strategic" joint ventures. For example, whereas Janger's 1980 survey of joint ventures (Janger, 1980) shows approximately 36% of respondents listing government restrictions as a major motive for establishing their joint ventures, our survey of more recent joint ventures (formed between 1986 and 1992) shows only 7% of respondents listing government restrictions as a major motive. Similarly, Janger's study shows approximately 25% of respondents listing access to raw materials as a major motive, while in this study only 5% of respondents listed this as a major motive. Instead, many of the more recent joint ventures were formed in order to access a new product or technology (24% listed this as a major motive), to jointly develop a new product or technology (28%), or to access managerial expertise (23%). Participants in Janger's survey did not list any of these motives as major reasons for forming their joint ventures.

As Harrigan (1988) suggests, joint ventures are now often used to obtain or supplement competitive strengths such as technological capabilities, management or marketing skills. Certainly, in recent years several factors have come to bear upon firms, requiring the use of creative approaches to building and leveraging capabilities (Lynch, 1989). These include:
- shorter product life cycles, which require firms to bring products to market at a quicker pace
- technology changes and "hybridization of technologies" (generic technologies such as laser disk technology are combined with other technologies to find applications in a variety of industries like music, video, and information services).
- a trend toward increased development costs, increasing the risks to firms undertaking the large expenditures required

Furthermore, many industries are becoming increasingly global in nature, requiring firms to coordinate actions across several markets to maintain competitive advantage (Yip, 1992). Especially in Europe, where markets are rapidly becoming more integrated, firms often pursue alliances to achieve consolidation through cooperation rather than "attack in the hope of winning" (Urban and Vendemini, 1992). Thus, there now appears to be a much broader variety of reasons why firms form joint ventures, which may account for the explosion of activity noted above.

The purpose of our study is to examine a large sample of these "new" and "strategic" alliances in order to determine whether they create shareholder value. We also aim to examine why some ventures create value while others don't.

2. Value-creation by joint ventures

Do joint ventures (domestic and international) create value for their U.K. parent firms? We try to answer this question by looking at shareholder benefits from the announcement of new joint ventures. Abnormal returns to shareholders are used as a measure of the stock-market's ex-ante expectations of joint venture performance. The analysis will test the proposition that:

Proposition = The abnormal returns associated with joint venture formation will be positive and significant for the U.K. parent firms involved.

A.   Evaluation methods

The sample for this analysis includes joint ventures, involving one or more U.K. parents, formed and announced during the period 1986 and 1992. Each joint venture announcement had to be referenced in the *Financial Times* Index with no confounding announcements made within plus or minus ten days of the announcement date. Also, stock returns information for at least one parent had to be available through Extel's MicroView + services for a minimum of 190 trading days (270 days were collected for most observations) prior to the announcement and 30 trading days after. The resulting sample consists of 235 observations relating to 213 joint ventures.

The analytical method used to test the impact of joint ventures announcements on shareholder wealth was the standard residual analysis technique or event-study methodology based on a market model as described by Fama (1976) and Brown and Warner (1985). Daily returns were used in this analysis (as opposed to monthly returns used in some studies of strategic events) so as not to capture the impact of other extraneous events which might outweigh the joint venture formation. The date on which the initial joint venture announcement appeared in the *Financial Times* was numbered as event day t = 0, with prior trading days numbered t =-1, t =-2, etc. and subsequent trading days numbered t =+1, t =+2, etc. The model estimates the expected returns for a joint venture parent firm based on the market return and the historical relationship of that firm's stock to the market, as follows:

(EQ 1)

$$R_{it} = a_i + b_i R_{mt} + e_{it}$$

where:

- R_{it} is the daily stock return for firm i on day t;
- R_{mt} is the daily return on the market portfolio on day t. In this study, the FT-A All Share index (an equally-weighted index of firms listed on the London Stock exchange) from the Micro View + database was used.
- a_i (alpha) and b_i (beta) are ordinary-least-squares estimates of the parameters of the relationship between the return on the firm's security and the market return.
- e_{it} is the error term, which is assumed to have a normal distribution and a mean value equal to zero.

The alpha and beta parameters were estimated for each firm i over the period - 270 to -91 trading days, and these parameters were then used to estimate the expected returns over the announcement period to be examined (Where information on a full 270 trading days prior to announcement was unavailable, a minimum of 190 days was considered acceptable). The difference between the actual returns and the expected returns for a firm on a given day, or the abnormal returns (AR_{it})were calculated as follows):

(EQ 2)

$$AR_{it}=R_{it}-(\hat{a}_i+b_iR_{mt})$$

Where: $\hat{a}$ and b are the parameters estimated for alpha and beta.

Abnormal returns for a two-day announcement period were examined for each joint venture. While day t $=0$ is the announcement date in the *Financial Times*, the actual news of a joint venture is often released the previous day. This two-day announcement period, therefore, is a cumulative abnormal return (*CAR*), where:

(EQ 3)

$$CAR_{i(-1,0)}=\sum_{t=-1}^{0} AR_{it}$$

For a sample of N securities, the average cumulative abnormal return was also calculated as follows:

(EQ 4)

$$\overline{CAR}(-1,0) = (\frac{1}{N}) \sum_{i=1}^{N} CAR_{i\ (-1,0)}$$

This average CAR for the sample as a whole was used to determine whether the joint venture announcements have a significant effect on the returns to shareholders of the U.K. parent firms. A t-statistic of statistical significance for the average CAR over N observations in the sample is calculated as follows:

(EQ 5)

$$t = \frac{CAR(-1,0)}{S_{CAR(-1,0)}/\sqrt{N}}$$

where: $S_{CAR(-1,0)}$ is the standard deviation of the two-day abnormal returns.

Thus, if the average CAR is positive and statistically significant it implied that the market expects the joint ventures, on average, to create value for the shareholders involved. If the average CAR is negative and statistically significant, the market expects that the joint ventures will actually destroy value. The methodology used, therefore, captures the market's perception of the long-run impact of the joint venture on the parent firms' cash flow. While the market's prediction at the time of announcement many not always reflect the actual realized performance of the joint venture in the future, it nevertheless should be unbiased (Linn and Rozeff, 1984). Furthermore, for events such as mergers it has been shown that abnormal returns at the time of announcement are highly correlated with increases in post-merger operating cash flows (Healy at al, 1992).

B.   Results

Daily returns and cumulative abnormal returns (*CARs*) for the full sample over the period (-10, +10) are reported in Table 1 along with a graph of the *CARs* (see figure 2). Table 2 shows *CARs* for different time windows. The mean two-day abnormal return for the 235 observations in the sample is 0.76% which is positive and statistically significant at the 5% level. Therefore, we can conclude that, on average, joint ventures do create shareholder value for the U.K. parent firms involved.

This positive result is consistent with earlier studies of U.S. domestic joint ventures (McConnell and Nantell, 1985; Koh and Venkatramen, 1991; Balakrishnan and Koza, 1993) as well as some studies of international joint ventures involving U.S. firms (Lummer and McConnell, 1990; Crutchley, Guo and Hansen, 1991; and Hu, Chen and Shieh, 1992). The magnitude of the reaction is also comparable to many existing studies. For example, in their studies of U.S. domestic joint ventures, McConnell and Nantell (1985) show a *CAR* of 0.73% for a two-day response time and Koh and Venkatramen (1991) show 0.87%. The results of this study are also within the range of findings from some other recent studies of international joint ventures. For example Lummer and McConnell (1990) show a two-day *CAR* of 0.40% for international joint ventures involving at least one U.S. parent; Chen, Hu, and Sheih (1992) find a two-day *CAR* of 1.22% for U.S firms forming international joint ventures. Crutchley, Guo and Hansen (1991) use a week-long response period in their study of U.S.-Japanese joint ventures and find that the U.S. parents receive an average *CAR* of 1.05%, and the Japanese parents receive an average *CAR* of 1.08%.

The positive results, however, differ from the results of some other studies of domestic and international joint ventures. For example, a study conducted by Finnerty, Owers and Rogers (1986) finds no evidence of significant abnormal returns upon the announcement of either domestic or international joint ventures. Lee and Wyatt (1990) find that, on average, investors react negatively to joint ventures with foreign firms. They show a CAR of 1.38% for an eleven-day test period starting with day -5 and ending with day 5. Chung, Koford and Lee (1993) also show a negative reaction to international joint ventures using a ninety-one-day test period extending from day-60 through day +30.

To test the sensitivity of our results to the time window chosen, we also examined the abnormal returns generated over a variety of time windows. The extended analysis shows no significant results for the period (-50, 4) and (1, 30). Therefore we can conclude that the window of analysis used in this study, which looks at abnormal returns from day -10 through day +10, is appropriate.

Table 1: Abnormal returns surrounding joint venture announcements

Day	Abnormal Return (AR)	Cumulative Abnormal Return (CAR)
-10	0.0009	0.0009
-9	0.0064	0.0073
-8	0.1183	0.1256
-7	0.1377	0.2633
-6	0.0433	0.3066
-5	-0.0461	0.2605
-4	0.0967	0.3572
-3	0.3400***	0.6972
-2	0.2288	0.9260
-1	0.5844**	1.5104
0	0.1797	1.6901
+1	0.0864	1.7765
+2	-0.0265	1.7500
+3	-0.0064	1.7564
+4	0.0902	1.8465
+5	0.0797	1.9263
+6	-0.0090	1.9173
+7	-0.0352	1.8821
+8	-0.0540	1.8281
+9	-0.0341	1.7940
+10	0.1079	1.9019

*p<0.10
**p<0.05
***p<0.02

Figure 2: Cumulative abnormal returns surrounding JV announcement

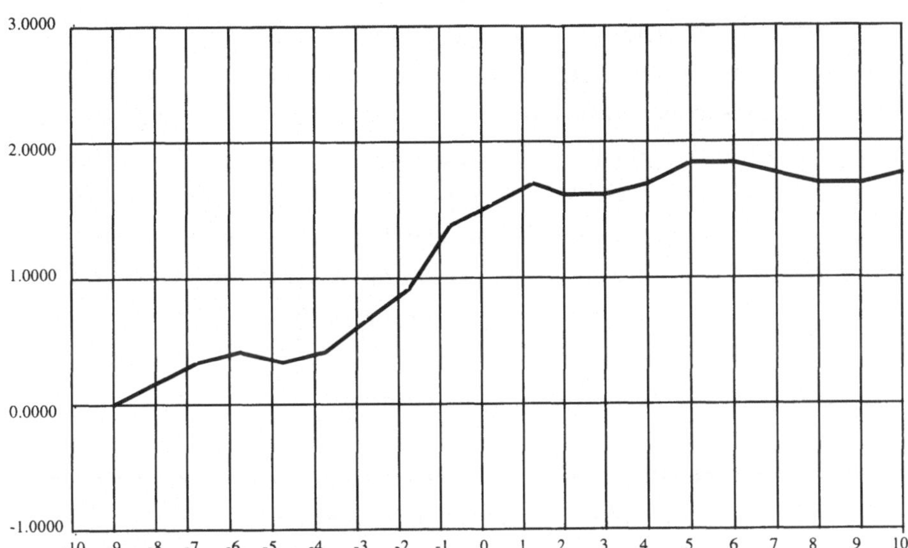

Table 2: Cumulative abnormal returns for various time windows

Window	CAR	t-statistic
CAR (-1,0)	0.76%	2.00**
CAR (-3,0)	1.33%	2.96***
CAR (-10,-1)	1.51%	2.97***
CAR (-10,-4)	0.36%	1.02
CAR (1,10)	0.21%	0.61

**p<0.05
***p<0.01

As Table 1 and Figure 2 show, the market's response seems to predate the newspaper announcement by a few days. However, no significant reactions prior to day -3 or after the announcement are evident. Therefore, although the reaction is occurring slightly earlier than expected, it appears that information is incorporated quickly - consistent with the assumption of an efficient capital market. The early response may indicate that companies are not as careful about leaking information regarding joint venture plans as they would be for acquisitions.

This may also be due to less rigorous enforcement of regulations on insider trading in England compared to the U.S. (Economist, 1993). Thus, for U.K joint ventures, the most appropriate response period may actually be a three- or four-day result starting with day -3. It is not uncommon for studies of international joint ventures to use a response period which is different from the standard two-day period used in most U.S.-based studies. For example Crutchley, Guo and Hansen (1991) use a week-long response period in their study of U.S.-Japanese joint ventures, Lee and Wyatt (1990) look at a 61-day test period, concentrating on days -5 through +5 and Chung, Koford and Lee (1993) use a 91-day test period, stretching from day -60 through +30.

C.   Domestic versus international joint ventures

Daily returns for domestic and international joint ventures are reported separately in Table 3. Figure 3 graphs *CARs* for the two groups.

The mean two-day abnormal return for international joint ventures is 0.80% and is significant at the 10% level; the mean two-day abnormal return for domestic joint ventures is 0.66%, but it is not statistically significant. However, as noted above, a more appropriate response time for this sample is a four-day response period starting with day -3. The *CARs* for the period from day -3 through day 0 are 1.28% for international joint ventures and 1.50% for domestic joint ventures. The results are significant at the 5% level for both groups, however analysis of variance indicates no significant difference between the two means.

Results for international joint ventures appear roughly similar to those for the sample as a whole, with a clean reaction just prior to the announcement date. However, the domestic group shows significant abnormal returns on several days surrounding the announcement date, particularly in the week or two prior to the announcement. This is difficult to explain, but it is possible this group yields some extraneous results because firms involved in domestic joint ventures often tend to be smaller, more thinly traded firms for which a market model using daily returns (as opposed to, perhaps, weekly or even monthly returns) is less appropriate. Another possible explanation is that early leakage of information may be more likely when the joint venture involves more than one domestic firm because there are most domestic firms from which information can emanate.

Table 3: Cumulative abnormal returns for domestic and international joint ventures

Window	Domestic	International
CAR (-1,0)	0.66%	0.80%*
CAR (-3,0)	1.50%**	1.28%*
CAR (-10,-1)	1.38%	1.55%***
CAR (-10,-4)	-0.09%	0.51%
CAR (1,10)	0.65%	0.07%

* P <0.10
** P <0.05
*** P <0.02

Figure 3: *CARS* – international vs. domestic joint ventures

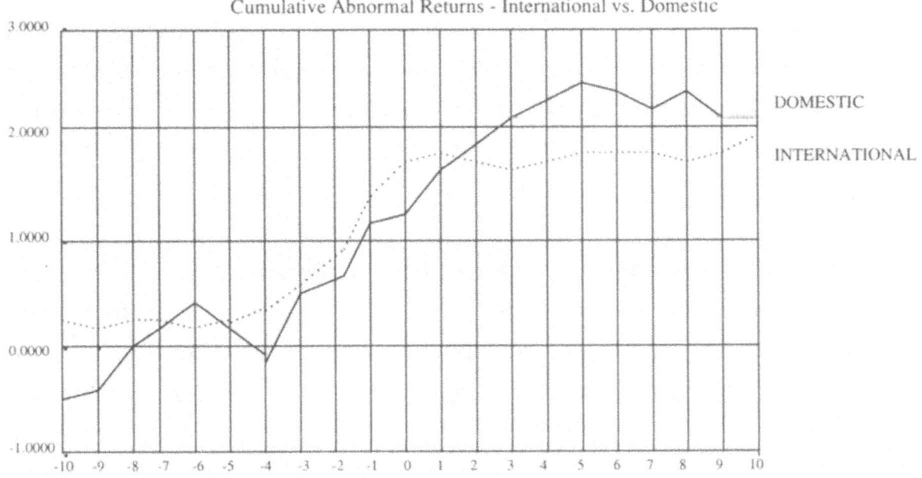

Whatever the explanation, it appears that market reacts somewhat differently to joint ventures depending upon whether they are domestic or international. While the magnitude of the reaction is similar, the timing is slightly different. Therefore in some of the analyses to follow it may be worthwhile to consider the two groups separately in addition to looking at the sample as a whole.

3.   Determinants of value

The event-study analysis in the previous section shows that, on average, joint ventures do create shareholder wealth. However, although the mean cumulative abnormal return (*CAR*) is positive, examination of the individual observations in our sample reveals that slightly more than half of the joint venture announcements are not accompanied by positive returns. What accounts for these variations in value? The current section seeks to answer this question through a more detailed analysis of the shareholder returns associated with joint ventures.

The valuation effects of joint ventures are likely to depend upon a number of factors, including characteristics of the parent firms involved, as well as features of the joint venture itself. For example, both Wild (1994) and Cordeiro (1993) have found a positive relationship between wealth creation in joint ventures and certain structural features of the ventures such as inside ownership, the presence of long-term performance plans, and higher numbers of director interlocks. Certainly other characteristics of the firms and their environment could have important effects. The nature of the joint venture partner's country, the industry environment, and the macroeconomic climate might all play a role.

There is now a huge academic literature that attempts to explain why some joint ventures create shareholder value while others do not. Rather then repeat all this literature here, we present in table 4 the main factors that this literature has identified as having an impact on shareholder value creation by joint ventures. In the same table we report what kind of relationship is proposed in the literature as well as the relationship we found from our empirical tests.

Our empirical test are based on a sample of 113 firms that responded to a questionnaire survey. The questionnaire was mailed to all 213 companies that we identified in the previous section of this paper and for which we had data on the abnormal returns generated by their joint venture announcement (the dependent variable). We received useable responses from 113 forms and this is the sample that forms the basis of our results from now on.

Table 4: Determinants of value: empirical findings

Independent Variable	Relationship Expected	Relationship Found
U.K. Parent Firm:		
possession of intangible assets	positive	negative
prior international experience	positive	negative
prior integration experience	positive	negative
profitability prior to joint venture	positive	negative
Partner Firm:		
state-owned entity	negative	negative
size of U.K. firm relative to partner	negative	non-linear
business related to U.K. parent	positive	none
Joint Venture:		
business related to U.K. parent	positive	positive
size relative to U.K. parent	positive	positive
prior ties between partners ("trust")	positive	negative
equal distribution of equity	positive	positive
equal distribution of voting rights	negative	negative
equal distribution of operating decisions	negative	negative
Partner Country:		
cultural "distance" between partners	negative	negative
integration of national capital markets	negative	none
government restrictions of joint venture	negative	negative
Industry Environment:		
industry concentration	non-linear	non-linear
industry growth rate	positive	none
Macroeconomic Environment:		
growth of British economy	positive	positive
strength of Pound sterling	positive	none

Of the several results that appear in table 4, we'd like to focus on one:

According to internalization theory (e.g. Hymer, 1960; Caves, 1971) firms go international so as to exploit intangible firm - specific assets (such as technology and brands), the markets for which are characterized by high transaction costs. Because of these high transaction costs, a firm cannot exploit its unique assets abroad unless it "internalizes" the market - hence the need for joint ventures.

If this explanation is valid, we would expect that the firms which benefit from international joint ventures will possess a lot of intangible assets (such as R&D or brands) and will have prior experience in exploiting these assets abroad. We would also expect that the more related the joint venture partner is to their business, the more effectively they will transfer their assets abroad. Finally, we would expect that since it is their technology and assets which are being transferred, they would have control over the venture, so that overall voting control is not important – they just dictate their terms anyway.

A look at table 4 suggests that all of the above predictions of internalization theory are not supported by our findings: possession of intangible assets as well as prior experience are negatively correlated to value creation by joint ventures; relatedness of partner has no relationship to value creation; and voting control in the venture appears to be important (since equal distribution of voting rights is negatively related to value creation).

What might explain these results? We believe that these results become less surprising if we look at joint ventures from a "learning" perspective. Suppose that the joint ventures are undertaken *not* to exploit firm-specific assets abroad but rather to learn and acquire somebody else's assets and skills. What relationships might we expect then?

The relationship that we should find once we take this learning approach to joint ventures are the following:

First, since the firm undertaking the joint venture is primarily interested in acquiring somebody else's skills and assets it doesn't really care if it has any assets itself – the firm wants its partner to have assets that it can acquire from him. Similarly, if the firm wants to learn new tricks, the partner must not be too related to the firm's existing business, otherwise there will be little room for learning new skills or things the firm doesn't already know. Finally, to maximise its learning from the venture, the firm needs to have control over it (such as voting control or control over operating decisions).

Thus, a learning perspective of joint ventures suggests that we should find a negative relationship between the firm's portfolio of intangible assets and value-creation; a negative (or insignificant) relationship between the relatedness of the partner and value-creation; and a positive relationship between having control of the venture and value creation. These are indeed the results we obtain in table 4, something which lends support to the learning perspective of joint ventures.

This perspective is also supported by what the managers themselves have stated in the questionnaires they filled out for us. When asked for their motive for forming a joint venture, several motives related to learning (such as accessing new technology or new managerial expertise) emerged as the major reasons for forming the venture.

The managers' rationale for forming the joint venture is reported in table 5. For each rationale, the first column lists the "percent mention" (the percent of respondents stating the motive was either a major reason or a minor reason for forming the joint venture). The second column lists the percent of respondents stating the motive was a major reason for establishing the joint venture. It should be noted that very few of the survey respondents were of the "old school" of joint ventures, established simply to extract raw materials, or because government restrictions required them to take partners. For example, in this sample, only 5% of joint ventures were established with a main motive being to extract raw materials. In an earlier study by Janger (1980) over a quarter of respondents listed this as a main motive. Similarly, in this study only 7% of respondents list government restrictions as a major reason for establishing the joint venture; in Janger's study this figure is more than one third.

Table 5: Rationale for joint venture formation

Rationale	% Major or Minor Reason	% Major Reason
Access Raw Materials	12	5
Access New Market	52	39
Access New Product or Technology	36	24
Access Managerial Expertise	50	23
Develop New Product or Technology	48	28
Achieve Economies of Scale	50	27
Integrate Vertically	19	9
Spread Risks	50	21
Establish Relationship	18	10
Co-opt Competitor	22	10
Block Competitor	21	6
Government Restrictions	18	7

For this sample, the most popular reason for establishing a joint venture is to access a new market for an existing product or technology. Over half of all respondents mention market access as either a major or a minor motivation, and nearly 40% list this as a major motive. This is not surprising; joint ventures have long been formed to access new markets. However, by examining the other major motives we bring some interesting points to light. Approximately 28% of all respondents cite the development of a new product or technology as a major reason for forming their joint venture, and nearly half (48%) mention it as either a major or a minor motivation. Half of all respondents mention access to managerial expertise as a reason for establishing the joint venture (with 23% citing it as a major reason). Significantly, over a third of respondents mention access to a new product or technology as a motive of the joint venture, with 24% listing it as a major motive. Clearly, this data is consistent with the idea that joint ventures are now being used to obtain and to supplement important competitive strengths (Porter and Fuller, 1986; Harrigan, 1988).

4.   Managerial assessments of joint venture performance

As a final exercise for this study, we also asked managers to rate the performance of their joint ventures. Survey participants were asked to give their assessments for a total of eight performance indicators. They were asked to rate performance against expectations for five specific parameters, and also for an overall assessment of performance. In addition, two indirect assessments of performance were requested. The eight performance parameters are the following:

AGAIN =   If your company had the opportunity to "do it all over again", would you engage in this joint venture?

ADDL =   Given the opportunity, would your company collaborate on additional projects with the same partner?

OVRLPERF =   Your overall assessment of how this joint venture performed relative to your expectation

SALESP =   Contribution of J.V. to sales

PROFP =   Contribution of J.V. to profits

TECHP =   Contribution of J.V. to technological expertise

MKTGP =   Contribution of J.V. to marketing capabilities

RISKP =   Contribution of J.V. to sharing of financial risk.

A correlation analysis for all eight performance indicators shows a very high degree of reliability and internal consistency (Cronbach Alpha=0.87), so we can be confident that the indicators are measuring the same thing. The overall performance rating (*OVRLPERF*) shows the highest correlation with total, thus it is a very good general indicator of performance for the joint ventures in this sample.

As shown in table 6, respondents' mean overall rating of joint venture performance was 3.06 indicating that, on average, performance met or slightly exceeded expectations. Thus the survey data provides support for the proposition:

Proposition: *Managers' assessments of joint venture performance, after the venture has been in operation for some time, will be positive.*

Table 6: Mean performance ratings – all measures

Measure	Rating on a scale of 1-5
AGAIN	3.93
ADDL	3.70
OVRLPERF	3.06
SALESP	2.86
PROFP	2.83
TECHP	3.12
MKTGP	3.04
RISKP	3.00

As shown in Table 7, the largest group of participants (44.2%) felt that their joint venture performed neither better, nor worse than expectations. For many (27.4%) the joint venture performed better than expectations, and a few (4.4%) were much better than expectations. 17.7% performed worse than expectations and 6.2% performed much worse. Therefore, approximately one third exceeded expectations and one quarter fell short. The other performance parameters also show ratings very close to expectations. It is interesting to note, however, that the more objectively measurable indicators of "contribution to sales" (*SALESP*) and "contribution to profitability" (*PROFP*) are slightly below expectations (2.86 and 2.83 respectively). The less objective measures of "contribution to technological expertise" (*TECHP*) and "contribution to marketing capabilities" (*MKTGP*) are slightly higher (3.12 and 3.04 respectively).

Table 7: Frequency distribution - overall performance measure

Rating vs. Expectations	Percent
Much Worse	6.2
Worse	17.7
Neither Better nor Worse	44.2
Better	27.4
Much Better	4.4

Another noteworthy point is that the indirect measures of performance scored fairly high. When asked the question: "Given the opportunity, would your company collaborate on additional projects with the same partner(s)?", approximately 68% of respondents felt that they would either "probably" or "definitely" collaborate on additional projects, about 13% were unsure, and 19% said they would "probably not" or "definitely not". When asked "If your company had the opportunity "to do it all over again" would you engage in this joint venture?", over 76% of respondents answered that they would "probably" or "definitely" engage in the joint venture, about 6% were not sure and the remainder (approximately 17%) answered that they would "probably not" or "definitely not". Thus is seems that while, on average, the joint ventures in our sample are meeting expectations, they are perhaps exceeding expectations when it concerns less tangible results (contribution to the firm's skills, or relationship with the partner firm) while they may fall short of more measurable and objective goals (sales and profitability).

5. Correlation between managerial assessments and cumulative abnormal returns

Some interesting results emerge when the managerial performance ratings of table 7 are compared to the stock market's reaction for each class of joint ventures (see table 8). Average cumulative abnormal returns do not seem to be related to managers' assessments. If anything, the cumulative abnormal returns appear to be higher for those joint ventures which managers consider to have performed worse than expectations, and lower for those which managers consider to have performed better than expectations.

Table 8: **Frequency distribution of overall performance plus average cumulative abnormal returns**

Rating	Percent	Avg.CAR (-1,0)	Avg.CAR (-3,0)
Much Worse	6.2	2.57	2.25
Worse	17.7	1.52	2.05
Neither	44.2	-0.35	0.32
Better	27.4	-0.09	0.78
Much Better	4.4	-0.30	0.73

Indeed, correlation analyses using both Pearson and Spearman correlation coefficients show no significant correlation between managers' assessments and either the two day or the four day *CARs*. (Pearson correlation coefficients are reported in Table 9.) In fact, it appears that there may be a slightly negative correlation between managers' assessments and the two day *CAR*.

Furthermore, cumulative abnormal returns do not correlate with the other specific performance measures provided by managers (with the exception of a positive correlation between CAR(-1,0) and MKTGP). This is in contrast to the findings of Koh and Venkatramen (1991) who compared abnormal market returns and managers' assessments of joint venture performance in the information technology sector and arrived at a Pearson correlation coefficient of 0.39

(p<0.01). It is also contrary to research by Geringer and Hebert (1991) which finds a positive and significant correlation between subjective and objective measures of joint venture performance. This brings into question whether the two measures of joint venture performance, abnormal returns and managers' assessments, are actually measuring the same thing.

Table 9: Correlation analysis

Pearson Correlation Coefficients / Prob > I R I under Ho: Rho=0

	OVRLPERF	CAR(-3,0)	CAR(-1,0)
OVRLPERF	1.0000 0.0000		
CAR(-3,0)	-0.0840 0.3828	1.0000 0.0000	
CAR(-1,0)	-0.1633 0.0883	0.8072 0.0001	1.0000 0.0000

Based on these results, we can conclude that, on average, investors expect joint ventures to perform well and according to managers, most of them do. However there does not appear to be any positive relationship between the two performance measures. In other words, while the average joint venture performs well using either measure, those individual joint ventures which the market expects to perform well are not necessarily the ones that do perform well according to managers. These results are extremely difficult to explain.

Three possible explanations exist for the lack of correlation between the two performance measures:

1. The stock market's reaction to some joint ventures may be biased.
2. Managers' assessments may be inaccurate or biased.
3. The market's expectations, and managers' assessments may be re-aligned over time.

A.   The stock market may be biased or inaccurate

The first basic argument listed above relates to one of the most heavily researched topics in corporate finance - the efficiency of the stock market. The majority of research on market efficiency supports the idea that the market is informationally efficient (Brealey and Meyers, 1988), meaning share prices reflect all publicly available information and respond rapidly to new information. In an efficient stock market, therefore, share revaluations for joint venturing firms should represent the capitalized value of any performance improvements resulting from those joint ventures. While the market may be efficient, on average, it is possible the market operates inefficiently for some joint ventures or exhibits some bias.

It is not within the scope of this study to provide extensive empirical evidence of market inefficiencies. However one source of bias or inaccuracies in the market could be bias in analysts' reports. As part of this study, brief interviews were conducted with industry analysts from top firms such as Goldman Sachs, James Capel, BZW and Country NatWest. Results of the interviews reveal that, while analysts tend to be very insightful, they are not necessarily systematic in the way they evaluate a company's joint ventures - particularly if the parent firms are small or if the joint ventures are perceived to be small or peripheral to the main business of the parent firms. In fact, one analyst admitted that when assessing international joint ventures, analysts are not always able to access the usual information sources and are often "led by the nose" by a parent firm's corporate finance executives.

To see if analysts (and therefore the market) show signs of bias, some brief analyses have been conducted. The correlation matrix from table 9 was recalculated for both the domestic and the international sub-samples. The correlation matrix was also repeated for joint ventures formed by large U.K parent firms (with market values greater than £500 million) versus joint ventures formed by small U.K parent firms (with market values less than £500 million).

We found no significant correlation between market performance measures and managers' assessments for either domestic or international joint ventures. However, the results for large versus small parent firms are revealing. For larger firms, the correlation between the market's expectations and managers' assessments is positive (although not significant), while for small firms the correlation is negative and significant. While there may be other plausible explanations for this phenomenon, one possibility is that the market is less accurate in assessing the future performance of joint ventures formed by small firms than it is in assessing those formed by their larger counterparts (most likely due to less thorough and accurate assessments by analysts who are naturally more attentive to larger market value firms). The market, therefore, may not be able to respond as efficiently to joint ventures formed by some firms (e.g. smaller firms). Thus the market's reaction to certain events may measure differences in information, rather than differences in firm performance. Again, there may be other explanations. While there appears to be some evidence of market bias, a more detailed investigation would be necessary before the phenomenon could be clearly understood.

B.   Managers may be biased or inaccurate

Another possible explanation for the disparity between the market's expectations and managerial perceptions is that managers themselves may be biased or inaccurate in their assessments. Particularly since managers' assessments are measured against prior expectations, it is possible that their assessments of performance or their recollection of prior expectations are biased. For example, some managers' expectations may have been unrealistically high, causing dissatisfaction - even with very good performance. Research in goal setting has shown that high expectations do serve to decrease satisfaction and positive outcomes serve to increase satisfaction through expectancy disconfirmation (Oliver et. al., 1994). It is also possible some managers can not accurately recall what their expectations for the joint venture had been - especially if their expectations-outcome consistency is an important moderator to hindsight bias and that hindsight bias is greater when outcomes are inconsistent with expectations (Schkade and Kilbourne, 1991).

In fact, most memory theorists agree all memories are inaccurate to some degree (Bartlett, 1932). Therefore, at least in some cases, it is entirely possible the measurement of performance against expectations is prone to bias.

C.   The two measures may become re-aligned over time

Finally, a third explanation for the discrepancy we are investigating is that the market's expectations and managers' assessments may be re-aligned over time based upon new information. Clearly, the market's reaction at the time of a joint venture's announcement will be a reaction to information available at that time. It will be based primarily upon the concept of the joint venture and its proposed strategy. However, a manager's assessment will also take into account the execution of that concept as well as any other information which becomes available after the announcement date. In the language of Mintzberg (1978), announcements are *intended strategies* which can be either *realized* or *unrealized.* Intended strategies are also frequently modified during implementation (Mintzberg and Waters, 1985; Quinn, 1980). As strategies evolve and are implemented, the *realized strategies* become more apparent. Based on new information about firm strategies, the market's assessments may come into alignment with managers' assessments over time. Furthermore, other types of information can simply be delayed in reaching the market. When the information becomes available, market assessments may change.

Again, a thorough exploration of the possibility of re-alignment lies outside the scope of this study. However, this is certainly a possibility that deserves further study.

Résumé

Les conséquences de l'évaluation des co-entreprises internationales

Les co-entreprises internationales s'inscrivent de plus en plus activement dans les nouvelles configurations organisationnelles - encore dénommées "alternatives" ou "hybrides" - d'un nouveau capitalisme ("Alliance Capitalism"). Ceci est vrai en particulier pour l'Europe, où, comme dans le reste du monde d'ailleurs, les partenariats sont de moins en moins d'ordre "tactique", mais deviennent délibérément "stratégiques". Compte tenu de l'augmentation de leur nombre on peut supposer que les co-entreprises sont source de création de valeur. Pourquoi ? Comment ? Dans quel mesure ? L'objet de cette étude est de fournir des réponses à ces questions en s'appuyant sur les réactions des marchés financiers et plus particulièrement sur la qualité des informations qu'ils génèrent et véhiculent. Le problème de la déformation de l'information, en particulier, est traité sous un jour nouveau.

Constantinos C. MARKIDES and Elizabeth A.M. TRACY

Zusammenfassung

Schlußfolgerungen aus der Evaluation von internationalen Joint-Ventures

Internationale Joint-Ventures sind alternative bzw. hybride Organisationsformen, die Teil eines neuartigen Kapitalismus ("Alliance Capitalism") sind. Dies gilt vor allem in Europa, wo - wie überall in der Welt - die Partnerschaften weniger "taktischen" als vielmehr bewußt "strategischen" Absichten entsprechen. Angesichts der Tatsache, daß ihre Anzahl steigt, liegt die Vermutung nahe, daß mit Hilfe von Joint-Ventures nennenswerte Wertschöpfungen entstehen. Warum? Wie? In welchem Maße? Die Autoren der Studie haben sich zum Ziel gesetzt, diese Fragen unter Einbeziehung der Reaktion der Finanzmärkte und ganz besonders der Qualität der durch sie hervorgebrachten und weitergeleiteten Informationen zu beleuchten. So wird das Problem der Verzerrung von Informationen in einem neuen Licht dargestellt.

References

BALAKRISHNAN, S./KOZA, M. (1993): Information Assymetry, Adverse Selection and Joint Ventures: Theory and Evidence. *Journal of Economic Behavior and Organization.* Vol 20. pp. 99-117.

BARTLETT, F. (1932): *Remembering: A Study in Experimental and Social Psychology.* Cambridge University Press. Cambridge.

BREALEY, R./MYERS, S. (1988): *Principles of Corporate Finance.* 3rd Edition. McGraw Hill. New York.

BROWN, S./WARNER, J. (1985): Using Daily Returns: The Case of Event Studies. *Journal of Financial Economics.* Vol 14. pp. 3-31.

CAVES, R. (1971): International Corporations: The Industrial Economics of Foreign Investment. *Economica.* February. pp. 1-27.

CHEN, H./HU, Y./SHIEH, J. (1991): The Wealth Effects of International Joint Ventures: The Case of U.S. Investment in China. *Financial Management.* Winter. pp. 31-41.

CHUNG, I./KOFORD, K./LEE, I. (1993): Stock Market Views of Corporate Multinationalism: Some Evidence from Announcements of International Joint Ventures. *The Quarterly Review of Economics and Finance.* Volume 33. Number 3 (Summer). pp. 275-293.

CONTACTOR, F. (1990): Ownership Patterns of U.S. Joint Ventures Abroad and the Liberalization of Foreign Government Regulations in the 1980s: Evidence from the Benchmark Surveys. *Journal of International Business Studies.* First Quarter. pp. 55-73.

CONTRACTOR, Fr. (1990): Contractual and Cooperative Forms of International Business: Toward a Unified Theory of Model Choice. *Management International Review,* 30 (1). pp. 31-54.

CORDIERO, J. (1993): The Role of Director Interlocks, Governance, and Management Incentives in Explaining Stockholder Gains from Joint Ventures. *Academy of Management Best Papers Proceedings 1993.* Atlanta. Georgia. pp. 12-16.

CRUTCHLEY, C./GUO, E./HANSEN, R. (1991): Stockholder Benefits from Japanese-U.S. Joint Ventures. *Financial Management.* Winter. pp. 22-30.

Datastream database.

ECONOMIST (1993): *Catching London's Culprits.* April 3. pp. 20.

EuroEquities database.

Extel Financial Analysts Service database.

FAMA, E. (1976): *Foundations of Finance.* Basic Books. New York.

Financial Times Index (1986-1992).

FINNERTY, J./OWERS, J./ROGERS, R. (1986): The Valuation Impact of Joint Ventures. *Management International Review*. Vol. 26. N° 2. pp. 14-26.

GERINGER, J./HERBERT, L. (1991): Measuring Performance of International Joint Ventures. *Journal of International Business Studies*. Quarter 2. pp. 249-263.

GERINGER, J./HERBERT, L. (1989): Control and Performance of International Joint Ventures. *Journal of International Business Studies*. Summer. pp. 235-254.

HARRIGAN, K. (1988): Joint Ventures and Competitive Strategy. *Strategic Management Journal*, 9. pp. 141-158.

HARRIGAN, K. (1988): Strategic Alliances and Partner Assymetries in International Business. in: *Cooperative Strategies in International Business*. edited by Contractor, F. and Lorange, P. Lexington Books, Lexington, Massachusetts, pp. 205-226.

HEALY, P./PALEPU, K./RUBACK, R. (1992): Does Corporate Performance Improve After Mergers? *Journal of Financial Economics*. Vol. 31. pp. 135-175.

HLADIK, K./LINDEN, L. (1989): Is an International Joint Venture in R&D for You? *Research Technology Management*. Volume 32. Number 4. July-August. pp. 11-13.

HLADIK, K. (1988): R&D and International Joint Ventures. in: *Cooperative Strategies in International Business*. edited by Contractor, F. and Lorange, P. Lexington Books. Lexington. Massachusetts. pp. 187-204.

HLADIK, K. (1985): *International Joint Ventures: An Economic Analysis of U.S.-Foreign Business Partnerships*. Lexington Books. Lexington Massachusetts.

HU, Y./CHEN, H./SHIEH, J. (1992): Impact of U.S.-China Joint Ventures on Stockholders' Wealth by Degree of International Involvement. *Management International Review*. Vol. 32. N° 2. pp. 135-148.

HYMER, S. (1960): *The International Operations of National Firms: A Study of Direct Foreign Investment*. Ph.D. Dissertation. MIT. published 1976 MIT Press. Cambridge, MA.

IFR, Securities Data, Thomson Financial Services.

INSEAD, Cooperative Ventures Database, INSEAD Accounting and Control Area.

JANGER, A. (1980): *Organization of International Joint Ventures*. Conference Board. Report # 787. New York.

KOH, J./VENKATRAMEN, N. (1991): Joint Venture Formations and Stock Market Reactions: An Assessment in the information Technology Sector. *Academy of Management Journal*. Vol. 34. N° 4. pp. 869-892.

LEE, I./WYATT, S. (1990): The Effects of International Joint Ventures on Shareholders Wealth. *Financial Review*. Vol. 25. N° 4. November. pp. 641-649.

LUMMER, S./McCONNELL, J. (1990): Stock Valuation Effects of International Joint Ventures. in: *Pacific-Basin Capital Markets Research*. edited by Rhee, S. and Chang, R.. Elsevier Science Publishers (North Holland). pp. 531-546.

LYNCH, R. (1989): *A Practical Guide to Joint Ventures and Corporate Alliances*. John Wiley and Sons. New York.

McCONNELL, J./NANTELL, T. (1985): Corporate Combinations and Common Stock Returns: The Case of Joint Ventures. *Journal of Finance*. Vol. 40. N° 2. June. pp. 519-536.

MINTZBERG, H. (1978): Patterns in Strategy Formulation. *Management Science*. May. pp. 934-948.

MINTZBERG, H./WATERS, J. (1985): Of Strategies Deliberate and Emergent. *Strategic Management Journal*. July-September. pp. 257-272.

OLIVER, R. et al. (1994): Outcome Satisfaction in Negotiation: A Test of Expectancy Disconfirmation. *Organizational Behavior and Human Decision Processes*. Vol. 60. N° 2. pp. 252-275.

PORTER, M./FULLER, M. (1986): Coalitions and Global Strategy, Competition in Global Industries. in: *Competition in Global Industries*. Porter, M.. Harvard Business School Press. Boston. Massachusetts. pp. 315-343.

QUINN, J. (1980): *Strategies for Change: Logical Incrementalism*. Irwin. Homewood, IL.

SCHKADE, D./KILBOURNE, L. (1991): Expectation-Outcome Consistency and Hindsight Bias. *Organizational Behavior and Human Decision Processes*. Volume 49. #1. pp. 105-123.

STOPFORD, J./WELLS, L. (1972): *Managing the Multinational Enterprise: Organization of the Firm and Ownership of the Subsidiaries*. Basic Books. London.

TEECE, D. (1992): Competition, Cooperation and Innovation: Organizational Arrangements for Regimes of Rapid Technological Progress. *Journal of Economic Behavior and Organization*. Vol. 18. pp. 1-25.

URBAN, S./VENDEMINI, S. (1992): *European Strategic Alliances: Co-operative Corporate Strategies in the New Europe*. Blackwell Publishers. Oxford. England.

WILD, K. (1994): *Managerial Incentives and the Valuation of International Joint Venture Formation*. University of London. Paper presented at the Academy of International Business Annual Meeting. November. Boston. Massachusetts.

YIP, G. (1992): *Total Global Strategy: Managing For Worldwide Competitive Advantage*. Prentice Hall. Englewood Cliffs. New Jersey.

Paolo Bertoletti

Economic Integration Effects on Market Structure

1.   Introduction

The way economists think about international trade and the gains of economic integration has significantly changed during the last two decades. The concept of comparative advantage, the beautiful and deep insight of David Ricardo, has not lost his theoretical relevance, and many analyses are still devoted to the way countries can exploit their differences by specializing and exchanging, and to the gains related to this inter-national and inter-industrial trade. However, several authors have come to focus on the international intra-industry trade (whose importance appears to be overwhelming in the case of developed countries), and on the role of the economies of scale in explaining it[1]. There are at least two reasons for this shift: first, the nowadays (and aforementioned) relevance of the intra-industry trade (for instance inside the European Union (EU)); second, the fact that some relatively recent advances in economic theory (and in particular in Industrial Organization) has eventually provided econo-mists with the analytical tools to cope with the inherent complexities of the increasing returns economics.

The story of the developing of the so-called "New Theory of International Trade" is a fascinating one, and it is (hopefully) not over yet[2]. However, it is fair to say that a cornerstone was the introduction into International Economics of the Chamberlinian model of differentiated products and increasing returns to scale, which had recently received sound microeconomics foundations[3]. This made possible and meaningful the study of the opening of trade between two "similar" and previously closed economies, and raised new interesting questions about the potential gains from trade and economic integration[4]. While the "Chamberlinian Approach" is not the only one which has been used to study the

---

[1]   See Krugman (1995).

[2]   See for instance the book by Krugman (1990).

[3]   The reference is respectively to the works by Krugman (1979) and Dixit and Stiglitz (1977).

[4]   For example: what does determine the international pattern of specialisation if resources and preferences are uniformly distributed? Is there a role for "first mover" effects and path dependency? Is free trade always the best policy?

several aspects of international trade, models of this kind proved able to provide a set of by now well-established results, and appear representative of the "New Theory"[5]. In this paper we focus on a version of such a model, and derive its main implications for the impact of integration on the market structure. Our goal is to lie down the point of view of the received economic theory about the main (stylized) effects of economic integration on a single industry. Simple as they turn out to be, we believe that its predictions can be usefully compared to the one stressed by other approaches, for instance to those considered by the business and management scholars. We hope therefore to contribute to the discussion among researches on what should be expected from the forthcoming completion of the EU internal market.

The paper is organized as follows: in section 2 we present the stylized model we want to consider. Section 3 summarizes its main implications. Section 4 introduces the possibility of firms cooperation (collusion). Section 5 contains a few final comments. The Appendix deals with some technicalities.

2. A brief look at the model

In this section we sketch the main components of a Chamberlinian model which follows the lines indicated by Krugman (1979) and (1980) in his two by now classical papers. That is, we consider an industry which is potentially composed by a large number N of distinct brands, each of them produced by a single firm whose output is denoted by X_i (here "large" means that $N > n$, where n is the number of operating firms) and whose price is p_i. Each firm has the same total cost function given by:

$$C(X_i) = F + cX_i,$$ (1)

where F is the amount of fixed costs, and c is marginal cost. That is, firms are identical and there are increasing returns to scale (internal economies of scale).

---

5   See e.g. Motta (1990).

It is assumed that consumers have "a taste for variety": namely, they like all brands and their tastes over the various brands are symmetric. In particular, we assume that there are L (identical) consumers concerned with the industry output (i.e. $X_i = Lx_i$), and that each of them has preferences which can be represented by the following (sub-) utility function:

$$U = -\frac{1}{\alpha}\sum_{i=1}^{N} e^{-\alpha x_i} = \frac{1}{\alpha}\left(n+1-N-\sum_{i=1}^{n} e^{-\alpha x_i}\right), \tag{2}$$

where x_i is brand i individual (per capita) consumption, and $\alpha > 0$. Note that utility is increasing in the number of purchased brands (i.e. $\partial U / \partial n > 0$). The utility function (2) satisfies the assumptions by Krugman (1990), p. 12: in particular, it is additively separable and, in an industry equilibrium (which implies $p_i = p$, and therefore $x_i = x$, $i = 1,n$), the (Allen-partial) elasticity of substitution between any of the brands ($\sigma = -1 / \alpha x$) is increasing in per capita consumption (decreasing in the price level p): see (A.6) in the Appendix[6]. Finally, for the sake of simplicity, we assume that consumers spend a fixed amount y of their income on the industry output [7].

Given the symmetry of our model, in any industry equilibrium it must be that $p_i = p$ and $x_i = x$, $i = 1,n$ (for economic feasibility, it must also be that $Y = Ly > F$, where Y is aggregate expenditure). To characterize the equilibrium industry configuration, in this paper we consider two alternative modes of competition: the case of monopolistic competition and the oligopoly equilibrium.

---

[6] This property gives rise to more pleasant results than the simpler assumption of a constant elasticity of substitution: see Krugman (1990), p. 18 and p. 27. However, the assumption of an elasticity of substitution decreasing in consumption is not, a priori, less plausible, and therefore this case should be investigated as well: the problem is that it gives rise to the possibility of multiple equilibria.

[7] In our partial equilibrium analysis, this is equivalent to assuming that each consumer uses a two-stage budgeting procedure in allocating his income (i.e., his preferences satisfy some separability assumptions), and that at the higher level the "aggregate" utility function has a Cobb-Douglas form: see e.g. Beath and Katsoulacos (1991), chapter 3.

A.   Monopolistic competition

We start by assuming that there are no barriers to entry, and that the equilibrium number of firms in operation is so large that each firm is of negligible size and can ignore the effect of its actions on the others[8]. This assumption, as it is well known, characterizes the Chamberlinian model of monopolistic competition (or "large" group equilibrium: see e.g. Beath and Katsoulacos (1991), pp. 42-43). As it is shown in the Appendix, in this case the industry equilibrium is determined by the following three conditions:

$$p = \frac{c}{1 - \alpha x},$$ (3)

$$p = c + \frac{F}{Lx},$$ (4)

$$p = \frac{y}{nx}.$$ (5)

Equation (3) is the profit-maximizing condition that marginal revenue equals marginal cost for each operating firm. Notice that, due to the assumption of an increasing elasticity of substitution between any of the brands, the mark-up $p/c - 1$ is an increasing function of the per capita consumption x. (4) is the zero-profit condition which must hold in a free-entry industry equilibrium. Equation (5) is simply the budget (accounting) condition that aggregate revenue equals expenditure: i.e., $npX = Y$ [9]. As it is shown in the Appendix, and it is explicit in equation (3), to get a consistent model (to satisfy the conditions for profit maximization, but without loss of generality) we restrict ourselves to the case where $x < 1/\alpha$. In such a case the schedules (3)-(5) are illustrated in Figure 1.

---

8   Implicitly, this requires that the fixed cost F is "small" with respect to the aggregate expenditure Y.

9   $X = Y/(np)$ can be thought of as Chamberlin's "DD" curve: i.e., the demand curve facing each firm when all firms change their prices simultaneously (see Beath and Katsoulacos (1991), p. 50).

Figure 1: The monopolistic competition equilibrium

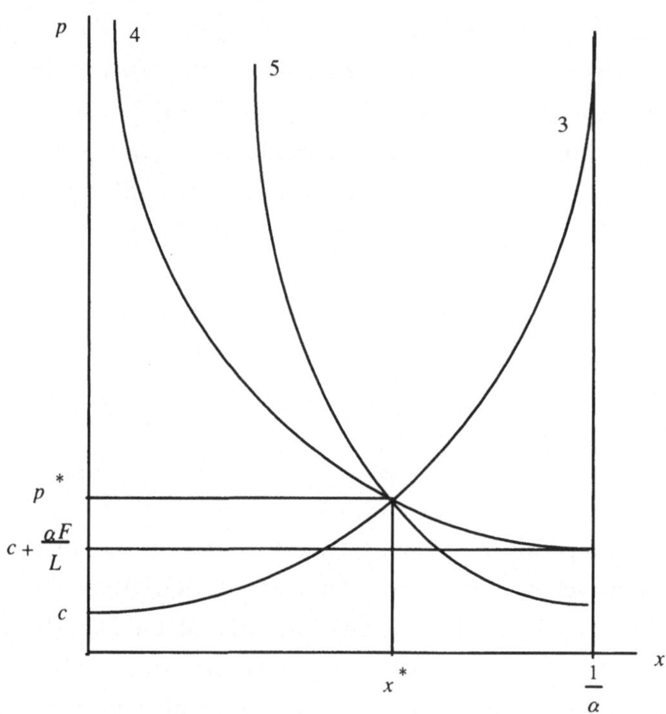

Note that, from Figure 1, an increase in L (the number of consumers), which shifts left the curve numbered four, implies a decrease in the equilibrium values p^* and x^*, and an increase in the number of operating firms[10]. By equation (4) we also see that the equilibrium output $X^* = Lx^*$ of each firm must also increase, as it should perhaps be expected. Therefore each consumer would benefit by an increase in the industry "market size" for two reasons: because it decreases the industry price and because it increases the number of available brands. These effects, of course, are due to the presence of increasing returns to scale, and to the assumption of free entry.

---

[10] As it is standard in literature, we are ignoring here the so-called "integer problem"; namely, the fact that a free-entry zero-profit equilibrium may not be consistent with an integer number of firms: see e.g. Beath and Katsoulacos (1991), p. 35.

B.   Oligopoly equilibrium

However, in assessing the impact of market integration, one can dispose of the free-entry assumption, at the cost of taking as exogenously determined the initial number of operating firms. In fact, in next section we will show that even if the industry entry is not free (e.g. because the fixed cost size is large enough to make the economies of scale act as an entry barrier) the effect of the opening of international trade is not qualitatively different. To build the background for this result, in this section we consider the Nash equilibrium of an oligopoly version of our model. In the Appendix it is shown that in this case the industry equilibrium, given the number of firms, is characterized by the profit-maximizing condition:

$$p = \frac{c(n - 1 + \alpha x)}{(n - 1)(1 - \alpha x)},$$
(6)

together with equation (5). Note that the firms number enters equation (6): this is due to the fact that each firm takes into account the impact of its action on the whole industry, whose configuration is determined by the number of operating firms. In particular, note that $\partial p / \partial n = - \alpha x / \left[(1 - \alpha x)(n - 1)^2 \right] < 0$: i.e., an increase in the number of firms has (perhaps obviously) a "pro-competitive" effect. This is so because when the brands number increases, the absolute value of each firm demand elasticity raises too (see (A.11) in the Appendix). Also notice that, once again, the mark-up $p / c - 1$ is an increasing function of x. The equilibrium is illustrated in Figure 2.

From Figure 2, an increase in the number of consumers does not modify the equilibrium industry price p^e, nor the individual consumption x^e, and thus it would only increase the output $X^e = Lx^e$ of each firm and of course its profits.

Figure 2: The oligopoly equilibrium

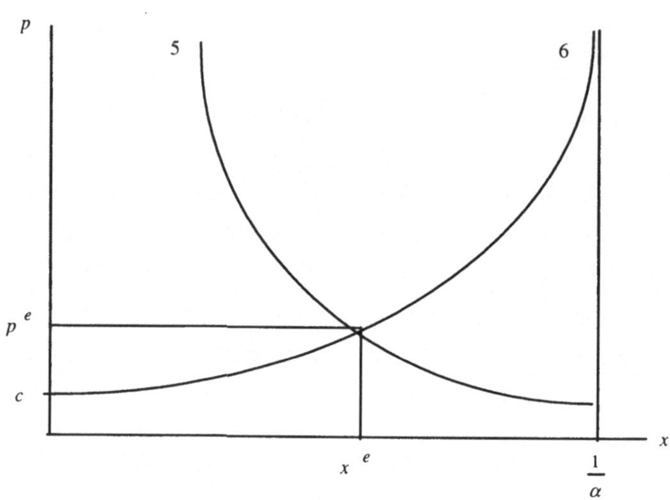

3. The effects of economic integration

A. Monopolistic competition

As indicated by Krugman (1979), and as far as the monopolistic competition model goes, the opening of international (intra-industry) trade between two similar economies can be summarized by saying that it is as if *each* country had experienced an increase in the number of consumers. Let us consider such an opening of trade. For the sake of simplicity, we assume that there are zero transportation costs, and that the two closed industries were identical. These assumptions immediately imply that the number of consumers doubles. Thus, the results of the previous analysis show that both the number of brands and the output of each firm raise, while price and per capita consumption of each brand decrease. Overall, the consumer surplus increases with respect to the case of autarky, and consumers get all the welfare gains from the opening of international trade (with monopolistic competition each firm earns zero profits). This is, of course, a re-statement[11] of the celebrated result by Krugman (1979).

---

[11] Krugman (1979) uses a general equilibrium model with one good and one input (labour).

In addition, we can also show that the ratio L/n^* increases: i.e., the brands number does not double. In fact, since by using (4) and (5) we get:

$$\frac{L}{n^*} = \frac{cX^* + F}{y} ,$$

(7)

an increase of the output X^* implies an increase in L/n^*. This means that, even if larger, the integrated industry cannot accommodate the same total number of firms as the two isolated ones. Thus, this model predicts that the economic integration will force some firms to leave the market. Since, in equilibrium, profits of the still operating firms remain zero, this implies that economic integration is hardly "good news" for the industry producers as a whole.

B. Oligopoly equilibrium

In this sub-section we show that even if the integrating industry were an oligopoly the impact of economic integration would not be different from what we saw above. Suppose first that the total number of firms does not change. In this case, an increase in the number of brands (firms double) decreases the price p^e. This effect of economic integration can be seen in Figure 2, since both curves shifts down. Moreover, by using (5) and (6), it is shown in the Appendix that $\partial x^e / \partial n < 0$: this means that the opening of international trade reduces each brand per capita consumption, very much as in the case of monopolistic competition. However, since by (5) the individual expenditure in each brand, $p^e x^e$, must reduce to a half (and since p^e reduces too), x^e does not halve. Thus $X^e = Lx^e$ increases, once again as in the monopolistic competition case. Finally, notice that the profits earned by each firm, $\pi^e = \left(p^e - c\right)X^e - F$, must decrease, since the revenue per firm Y/n is constant while each firm total cost $C\left(X^e\right) = F + cX^e$ increases.

Of course, it might be that the profit reduction forces some firm to leave the industry in order to avoid a negative return. In this case the number of operating firms increases but does not double, p^e and x^e decrease, and a zero-profit equilibrium get established. Also in this case, by (5), $p^e x^e$ must reduce, but this time it does not halve. Again, by using (4) one can see that this implies that the output x^e of each firm increases[12]. Thus, even in an oligopoly equilibrium[13], economic integration is a good piece of news for the consumers while it is certainly not so for the producers as a whole (very much as in the monopolistic competition case).

4. On the possibility of firms cooperation

The story told by our stylized model is extremely simple: since there are economies of scales in production, there are gains from the opening of international trade (through an increase in the firms size). Moreover, the end of autarky increases the competitive pressure and, even under imperfect competition, consumers appropriate the whole increase in welfare, while profits tend to decrease and some firms have to leave the market. Of course one might wonder whether the worsening of firms perspectives (the shock due to the end of autarky) may change the mode of their competition. This amounts to ask whether (in the oligopoly version of our model) firms may then find a way to pursue "co-operative strategies" to avoid the aforementioned unpleasant results. Of course, in our simple setting, "strategic cooperation" ought to mean some sort of tacit collusion, at the consumers' expense. Indeed, Chamberlin himself conjectured that the firms in an industry might be able to charge the monopoly price, even without an explicit agreement among them[14]. In the jargon of modern economic theory, this is equivalent to conjecturing the existence of a Nash equilibrium which sustains a more "collaborative" mode of firm competition than the one we have considered (i.e., an higher level of profits).

---

[12] To see this, note that (indicating the equilibrium variables of the integrated market with a tilde), the zero-profit property implies that $\tilde{p}^e \tilde{L}\tilde{x}^e = c\tilde{L}\tilde{x}^e + F$, while for the isolated industries $p^e Lx^e > cLx^e + F$. But, since $\tilde{L} = 2L$, by subtracting the former condition from the latter we get $0 > L\left(p^e x^e - 2\tilde{p}^e \tilde{x}^e\right) > c\left(x^e - \tilde{x}^e\right)$.

[13] One can easily show that the following proposition applies to the case of a free-entry (that is a zero-profit) oligopoly equilibrium as well.

[14] Here the reference is to the so-called Chamberlinian "small" group equilibrium: see e.g. Tirole (1988), pp. 239-240, and Beath and Katsoulacos (1991), p. 43.

However, in our static (one-shot) setting, there is a unique Nash equilibrium, and to get a form of firms cooperation we would need to consider a full-fledged dynamic model of repeated price interaction. In such a richer context, as it is well-known, firms could enforce several types of Chamberlinian tacit collusion, for example by the threat of retaliation (i.e., by using strategies which "reward" cooperation and "punish" deviations): see e.g. Tirole (1988), chapter 6. To construct a consistent dynamic version of the previous model is beyond the goal of this paper: here we limit ourselves to a few general considerations concerning a possible "supergame" extension of it, and the likely effect of economic integration. According to the supergame methodology, if firms repeatedly interact, and if, ceteris paribus, they are "patient enough" (i.e., if their intertemporal discount factor is sufficiently high), prices higher than the one given by (6) (and even the "monopoly price"[15]) can be sustained as a Nash equilibrium. In particular, a given "collusive" price $\bar{p}$ is sustainable in equilibrium if the discount factor δ of each firm is such that:

$$\delta \geq \frac{\tilde{\pi}(\bar{p}) - \pi(\bar{p})}{\tilde{\pi}(\bar{p}) - \underline{\pi}} = \delta^*(\bar{p}), \tag{8}$$

where $\pi(\bar{p})$ is the (per-period, collusive) equilibrium profit of each firm [16]. In (8), $\underline{\pi}$ is the profit which corresponds to a period of (maximal) punishment which would follow a deviation from collusive behaviour, and it can be safely normalized to zero (a firm can always exit the market), while $\tilde{\pi}(\bar{p})$ is the one-shot profit each firm would get from deviating and undercutting its price (note that it depends on the collusive price). Thus, the value of $\delta^*(\bar{p})$ summarizes the requirements for a sustainable collusion on $\bar{p}$.

Indeed, equation (8) allows the formalization of some aspects of the conventional wisdom on collusion (which goes back at least to the works of Chamberlin and

---

15   In our model, due to the simplifying assumption of a fixed expenditure y , the monopoly price is not well-defined since the "collusive" demand curve $X = Y / (np)$ has a unity price elasticity.

16   Formally, (8) applies to the case of an infinitely repeated price interaction: see Tirole (1988), paragraph 6.3.

Bain). For instance, according to it market dilution and increasing returns to scale hinder collusion, because they make undercutting more profitable. This is formalized in (8) through the value of δ^*, which is obviously an increasing function of the number of firms, and depends positively on the degree of returns to scale[17]. In other words, market concentration and decreasing returns to scale, by reducing the size of the discount factor required to sustain collusion, make it more likely. What does (8) tell us about the effect of economic integration? In our model the opening of international trade doubles both firms and consumers, and thus it raises the value of the discount factor required to implement any collusive price. In fact, while $\pi(\bar{p})$ is obviously unchanged, whatever $\bar{p}$ be, $\bar{\pi}(\bar{p})$ and then $\delta^*(\bar{p})$ are raised by the increase in the amount of consumers, and by the effect of the economies of scale. Thus, this suggests that economic integration might well benefit consumers also by making price collusion among firms more difficult[18].

5. Conclusions

In this paper we have used a Chamberlinian model of an industry, built along the lines indicated by the so-called "New Theory of International Trade", to investigate the main implications of the opening of trade between two previously closed economies. In short, our results stress that economic integration improves consumers welfare, and worsens the firms perspectives. In particular, international trade has an unambiguous "pro-competitive" effect. Consequently, profits reduce and/or some firms have to exit the market (though the "surviving" ones increase their size), and collusion among producers becomes more difficult. Moreover, these results accord closely with the widespread opinion among

---

[17] Consider for example a homogenous-good industry with n identical firms which all charge the monopoly price $\bar{p}$. Then with constant average costs one gets $\bar{\pi}(\bar{p}) \approx n\pi(\bar{p})$ and therefore $\delta^* \approx 1 - 1/n$, while with decreasing average costs to sustain collusion the discount factor must be even higher ($\bar{\pi}(\bar{p}) > n\pi(\bar{p})$ and $\delta^* > 1 - 1/n$): see Tirole (1988), pp. 247-248.

[18] According to the conventional wisdom on collusion, another direct way the opening of international trade can affect the possibility of firms collaboration might be by increasing the degree of industry heterogeneity: again see Tirole (1988), p. 242.

theoretical economists that an increase in the market size should put more competitive pressure on firms, and that in turn this should increase the general industry efficiency. Roughly, they seem also to correspond to the hopes of many about the positive effects of the internal EU market completion, and even to the movement toward concentration and mergers that the latter appears to have encouraged[19].

However, while we think it does constitute a useful benchmark, our stylized model is certainly both too simple and too limited to fully predict the ultimate effect of the European economic integration, and we do not pretend it should be taken as a unique guideline. In particular, our partial (one-industry) equilibrium analysis cannot substitute for a more general one. For example, our clear-cut prediction of the producers (as a whole) situation worsening may be challenged by the consideration that economic integration may also change the factor market conditions, perhaps lowering the production costs[20]. Analogously, while in our model cooperation among firms can only mean some sort of price collusion at the expense of consumers, in a richer context (think for instance of vertical relationships) it might serve efficiency, and even be in the consumers' interest; moreover, as regard that case, we have little basis to forecast the effect of economic integration[21].

But perhaps the main warning on a straightforward application of our model comes from the striking difference between its predictions on the worsening of firms perspectives and the ones put forward by the managerial and business literature on the creation of the European unified market. For example, one cannot read the stimulating book by Urban and Vendemini (1992) without

---

19 See e.g. Urban and Vendemini (1992), chapter 1.

20 It should be mentioned here that a challenge to this prediction might also come from the traditional "comparative advantages" approach to international trade, which implies that firms which survive to economic integration (inside the industry in which their economy specialises) improve: see e.g. Krugman and Obstfeld (1994), chapter 5.

21 However, if their perspectives do worsen, one should expect that firms cooperation becomes more difficult, since the value of having a reputation for collaborative behaviour decreases: see e.g. Milgrom and Roberts (1992), chapter 8.

being struck by their feeling that the European economic integration constitutes a huge opportunity for enterprises. And this is confirmed by the public declarations of many opinion leaders and businessmen who, presumably, explicitly think in terms of profits! Now, part of the explanation of such a difference comes from the fact that, from one point of view, the use of the Chamberlinian approach to discuss this particular topic (the firms perspectives in the unified Europe) is a bit unfair. As we have indicated, this particular model was developed in order to explain the actual pattern of international trade, and it has been successful in answering specific questions in international economics (see footnote 4). But, for example, to explain the optimism of a particular manager on economic integration may require that firms asymmetries and differences in efficiency are taken into account (i.e., it might be that a firm expects to gain from economic integration at the expense of other (less efficient) firms rather than of consumers, or even through an improved position in the external (to the integrated market) competition). Our symmetric model is certainly not well-equipped for this goal. In other words, economic theorists certainly know that market competition has many more aspects than those captured by the simplest of their models, and that more competitors can also means more opportunities of mutually beneficial "trade". That is, they know that firms do not only compete but also "complement" each other: see e.g. Nalebuff and Brandenburger (1996), chapters 1 and 2. However, part of the indicated difference between what we may call "the point of view of economists" and the management and business scholars' expectations remains puzzling, and deserves more attention. We hope that this paper can serve to illustrate such a difference, and that it can stimulate a debate on it.

6.   Appendix

This section presents some analytical results on the model we use in this paper. To start with, we wish to show that the utility function in (2) implies that in an industry equilibrium ($p_i = p$ and $x_i = x$, $i = 1,n$) the Allen-partial elasticity of substitution between any of the goods ($\sigma_{i,j}$, $i,j = 1,n$) are equal to $-1 / \alpha x$. To prove this, consider the following first-order conditions of utility maximization:

$$\frac{\partial U}{\partial x_i} = e^{-\alpha x_i} = \lambda p_i, \qquad\qquad i = 1, n, \qquad\qquad (A.1)$$

where the positive Lagrange multiplier λ measures the marginal utility of income. From (A.1), one immediately get the familiar condition that the marginal rate of substitution between any two brands equals their relative price:

$$e^{-\alpha(x_i - x_j)} = \frac{p_i}{p_j}, \qquad\qquad i = 1, n, \qquad\qquad (A.2)$$

and, after some computation, the following individual demand functions:

$$x_i(p_1,\ldots,p_n,y) = \frac{1}{\alpha \sum\limits_{j=1}^{n} p_j}\left(\alpha y - \sum_{j=1}^{n} p_j \ln\frac{p_i}{p_j}\right), \qquad i = 1, n \qquad (A.3)$$

(note that, from (A.3), in an industry equilibrium $x_i = y / (np) = x$). Analogously, one can use (A.1) to derive the following "Hicks-compensated" demand functions:

$$\bar{x}_i(p_1,\ldots,p_n,u) = \frac{1}{\alpha}\left[\ln\sum_{j=1}^{n} p_j - \ln p_i - \ln(n+1-N-\alpha u)\right], \qquad i = 1, n, \qquad (A.4)$$

where u is the utility level, and in turn the expenditure function:

$$E(p_1,\ldots,p_n,u) = \sum_{j=1}^{n} p_j \bar{x}_j = \frac{1}{\alpha}\sum_{i=1}^{n} p_i\left[\ln\sum_{j=1}^{n} p_j - \ln p_i - \ln(n+1-N-\alpha u)\right]. \qquad (A.5)$$

Eventually, one can compute (see e.g. Takayama (1986), pp. 144-145) from (A.4) and (A.5) that in an industry equilibrium:

$$\sigma_{i,j} = \frac{E}{\bar{x}_i \bar{x}_j}\frac{\partial \bar{x}_i}{\partial p_j} = \frac{-1}{\alpha x} = \sigma, \qquad\qquad i,j = 1, n. \qquad\qquad (A.6)$$

We now turn to the derivation of conditions (3)-(5). Consider back (A.1): it implies that:

$$x_i = \frac{-1}{\alpha}\left[\ln\lambda + \ln p_i\right], \qquad\qquad i = 1, n. \qquad\qquad (A.7)$$

The monopolistic competition assumption of a large number of firms with negligible size can be turned into the fact that each firm pricing policy has a null effect on the marginal utility of income (see e.g. Krugman (1990), pp. 13-14).

219

This means that one can obtain the elasticity of the demand facing each firm directly from (A.7). Namely:

$$\varepsilon_i = \frac{\partial x_i}{\partial p_i}\frac{p_i}{x_i} = \frac{-1}{\alpha x_i} \qquad\qquad i = 1, n. \qquad\qquad (A.8)$$

Notice that, as noted by Krugman (1990), p.12-14, $\varepsilon_i = x_i(\partial U / \partial x_i) / (\partial^2 U / \partial x_i^2)$, due to the additivity of the utility function (2). Moreover, in an industry equilibrium, $\varepsilon = \sigma$. Consider now the profit maximization problem of each firm. Since firm profits are given by $\pi_i = (p_i - c)x_i - F$, it is easily verified that the first-order condition requires:

$$p_i = \frac{|\varepsilon_i|}{|\varepsilon_i| - 1}c = \frac{c}{1 - \alpha x_i}, \qquad\qquad (A.9)$$

with $|\varepsilon_i| > 1$. This happens if and only if $1 > \alpha x_i$, and we restrict our attention to this case (there is no loss of generality, since we can "exploit" the degree of freedom offered by α to accommodate any level of x)[22]. This explains condition (3) (note that the mark-up is equal to $|\varepsilon_i| / (1 - |\varepsilon_i|)$, and thus it is increasing in x_i under our assumptions). Condition (4) is simply the zero-profit (free-entry) condition $\pi_i = 0$. Finally, (5) simply states the budget condition $\sum_{i=1}^{n} p_i x_i = y$ for an industry equilibrium.

To establish (6), one needs to compute the "true" demand elasticity from (A.3).

This gives:

$$\varepsilon_i = \frac{p_i - \sum_{j=1}^{n} p_j}{\alpha y - \sum_{j=1}^{n} p_j \ln\frac{p_i}{p_j}} - \frac{p_i}{\sum_{j=1}^{n} p_j}, \qquad\qquad i = 1, n, \qquad\qquad (A.10)$$

which reduces to:

$$\varepsilon = -\frac{n - 1 + \alpha x}{\alpha n x} \qquad\qquad (A.11)$$

---

[22]   The second-order condition is satisfied if $\alpha x_i < 2$.

in an industry equilibrium. Note that $\varepsilon > -1/(\alpha x)$ (and $|\varepsilon| > 1$) if $1 > \alpha x_i$. Moreover, $\partial \varepsilon / \partial n < 0$. From the first equality in (A.9) one eventually gets (6).

As the last step, let us prove that (5) and (6) imply that $\partial x^e / \partial n < 0$. Together, they give:

$$nx^e c\left(n - 1 + \alpha x^e\right) - (n - 1)\left(1 - \alpha x^e\right)y = 0, \tag{A.12}$$

and thus, by differentiating:

$$\frac{\partial x^e}{\partial n} = -\frac{x^e c\left(n - 1 + \alpha x^e\right) + nx^e c - \left(1 - \alpha x^e\right)y}{nc\left(n - 1 + \alpha x^e\right) + \alpha nx^e c + \alpha(n - 1)y}. \tag{A.13}$$

From (A.13), $sign\left\{\partial x^e / \partial n\right\} = sign\left\{\left(1 - \alpha x^e\right)y - x^e c\left(n - 1 + \alpha x^e\right) - nx^e c\right\}$, and some additional computations (by using again (5) and (6)) show that $sign\left\{\partial x^e / \partial n\right\} = sign\left\{f(n) = n^2 - 2n + 1 - \alpha x\right\}$, which is positive since $f(\cdot)$ is so for $n \geq 2$ and $1 > \alpha x_i$.

Paolo BERTOLETTI

Résumé

Effets de l'intégration économique sur la structure des marchés

Ce chapitre analyse les effets de l'intégration économique sur la structure de marché et donc les gains potentiels des consommateurs et des producteurs, en utilisant un modèle inspiré d'Edward Chamberlin (Harvard). Le cadre est celui - très réaliste - d'une concurrence imparfaite, plus précisément celui d'une industrie avec produit différencié. Le marché reste-t-il dès lors une source d'information ? La question est pertinente dans le contexte d'une intégration économique telle qu'elle est vécue par l'Union Européenne où s'expriment de nombreuses situations de concurrence monopolistisque, d'oligopole, de collusion coopérative. L'ouverture intensifiée au commerce international, la présence de rendements d'échelle croissants, l'augmentation des variétés produites, la baisse des prix sont des facteurs qui fragilisent les entreprises par la réduction des profits, voire la contrainte de sortie du marché. La conduite des entreprises dans un contexte de comportements flous des acteurs est rendue plus difficile que ne le suggère les modèles d'analyse théoriques, et que contestent les managers ou les entrepreneurs. Les choix décisionnels restent à gérer en information imparfaite croissante compte tenu de la complexité des jeux.

Zusammenfassung

Auswirkungen der wirtschaftlichen Integration auf die Struktur der Märkte

In diesem Beitrag werden die Auswirkungen der wirtschaftlichen Integration auf die Struktur der Märkte und damit die potentiellen Vorteile für Verbraucher und Produzenten untersucht. Dabei wird ein von Edward Chamberlin (Harvard) inspiriertes Modell genutzt. Die angenommenen - sehr realistischen - Rahmenbedingungen sind die einer unvollständigen Konkurrenz, genauer gesagt einer Industrie mit differenzierten Produkten. Ist in einer solchen Situation der Markt weiterhin Informationsquelle? Diese Frage ist von herausragender Bedeutung gerade im Zusammenhang mit wirtschaftlicher Integration, wie sie sich in der Europäischen Union abspielt, wo zahlreiche Wettbewerbssituationen wie Monopole, Oligopole und kooperative Konkurrenzsituationen nebeneinander existieren. Die immer weitere Öffnung zum Weltmarkt, die wachsenden Skalenerträge, die Zunahme der Produktvielfalt, die Preissenkungen führen zur Schwächung der Unternehmen über den Rückgang der Gewinne, wenn nicht gar zum Ausstieg aus dem Markt. Die Unternehmensführung bei unklaren Verhaltensweisen anderer Akteure wird in stärkerem Maße erschwert, als die theoretischen Analysemodelle dies nahelegen und Führungskräfte und Unternehmer zugeben. Die Entscheidungsprozesse müssen angesichts der Komplexität der Situationen bei wachsender Informationsunsicherheit durchgeführt werden.

References

BEATH, J./KATSOULACOS, Y. (1991): *The Economic Theory of Product Differentiation*. Cambridge University Press. Cambridge.

DIXIT, A.K./STIGLITZ, J.E. (1977): Monopolistic Competition and Optimum Product Diversity. *American Economic Review*. Vol. 67. pp. 297-308.

KRUGMAN, P.R. (1979): Increasing Returns, Monopolistic Competition, and International Trade. *Journal of International Economics*. Vol. 9. pp. 469-479. Reprinted in: Krugman, P.R. (1990): pp. 11-21.

KRUGMAN, P.R. (1980): Scale Economies, Product Differentiation, and the Pattern of Trade. *American Economic Review*. Vol. 70. pp. 950-959. Reprinted in : Krugman, P.R. (1990): pp.22-37.

KRUGMAN, P.R. (1990): *Rethinking International Trade*. MIT Press. Cambridge (MA).

KRUGMAN, P.R. (1995): Increasing Returns, Imperfect Competition and the Positive Theory of International Trade. Chapter 24. in: Grossman, G. and Rogoff, K. (Eds.): *Handbook of International Economics*. Vol. III. pp. 1243-1277. North-Holland. Amsterdam.

KRUGMAN, P.R./OBSTFELD, M. (1994): *International Economics* (third edition). Harper Collins. New York.

MILGROM, P./ROBERTS, J. (1992): *Economics, Organization and Management*. Prentice Hall. Englewood Cliffs.

MOTTA, M. (1990): Recent Models of International Trade and Distributional Gains from Integration. *Rivista Internazionale di Scienze Economiche e Commerciali*. Vol. 37. pp. 713-736.

NALEBUFF, B.J./BRANDENBURGER, A.M. (1996): *Co-opetition*. Harper Collins. London.

TAKAYAMA, A. (1986): *Mathematical Economics* (second edition). Cambridge University Press. Cambridge.

TIROLE, J. (1988): *The Theory of Industrial Organization*. MIT Press. Cambridge (MA).

URBAN, S./VENDEMINI, S. (1992): *European Strategic Alliances*. Blackwell. Oxford.

Hanns A. Abele

Asymmetric Information as a Problem for Financing Small or Medium Size Enterprises

1. Introduction

2. National systems for financing innovation and SME

3. Some observations on the role of asymmetric information in financial intermediation
   A. Actors
   B. Basic assumptions
   C. Some results

4. Conclusions

---

1. Introduction

Despite a number of objections GDP per head is an established measure of the wealth of nations. Consequently the rate of economic growth is used as an indicator of increases in economic welfare. At an aggregate level it is clear that an increased use of inputs and/or a higher productivity of the production process are basic ingredients for economic growth.

Among the first group one may concentrate on increases of the capital stock besides population growth (and migration) implying increased labour supply. Investment comes out as a strategic factor of economic growth, which is in essence the message of the so-called Harrod-Domar theory of growth. As a long run extension of the income effect of the Keynesian multiplier this growth model integrates the capacity effect of investment. By definition investment is a change in real capital stock which extends production possibilities.

Using an aggregate production function of the Cobb-Douglas type this argument is easily illustrated.

$$Y_t = A_t^{\lambda} K_t^{\alpha} L_t^{1-\alpha}, 0 < \alpha < 1 \quad (1)$$

Y being GDP, A a technology (shift) parameter, K capital input, L labour input, $\acute{a}$ the production elasticity of capital, and $\ddot{e}$ the rate of technological progress. Taking logarithms and the time derivative leads to (2) where lower case letters symbolise growth rates

$$y = \lambda a + \alpha k + (1 - \alpha)l \quad (2)$$

(2) is an equation showing the rate of growth of GDP being a weighted sum of technological parameters, technological progress and the growth of factor inputs.

Population growth is typically rather small in industrialised countries, but migration in several forms may increase the labour force. On the other hand investment does not only increase capital stock but turns out to be the vehicle for technological progress to enter the production process.

Thus technology emerges as the key factor for economic growth and the wealth of nations. What determines the rate of technological progress? Usually one distinguishes invention and innovation as the key steps towards new products and processes. Whereas the process of discovery seems to be very difficult to influence being more mysterious and, moreover, dependent on luck and a favourable environment, policy measures concentrate on innovation, that is the economic exploitation of the ideas created by investors. Consequently research has focused on factors creating a speedy transformation of knowledge into economic gains. The importance of the technology race was underlined by the final developments in the cold war area which made clear that the collapse of the Eastern regimes was accelerated by their inability to keep up with the Western pace of technological development.

Although large enterprises, very often transnational enterprises, are important for the development of markets and standard setting they often tend to retard further development. This is in part a consequence of their market position as monopolists or oligopolists, in part an implication of their amount of capital invested and thus of their level of sunk costs. Recent examples of this hypothesis are the steel industry especially the so-called LD-process[1] or the rise of the personal computer industry and the interplay of IBM and Microsoft and Intel respectively. Normally small firms and especially start up companies lack the necessary capital to develop new markets or to successfully launch an assault on existing markets.

One of the important sources of economic dynamics in any economy are small and medium-sized enterprises (SME). Because of their great flexibility they can move into new production processes and new products much faster than large enterprises. They can afford riskier strategies because their loss potential is limited.

---

[1]   See Adams, Dirlam (1966), (1967), and Mc Adams (1967).

However, they may have disadvantages with respect to their marketing capabilities or finance opportunities. From a theoretical perspective this shifts the focus away from traditional growth theory to the study of the impact of money and finance[2] and market structure on economic growth. The latter areas are the realms of the theory of finance and industrial economics.

2. National systems for financing innovation and SME

Having identified finance as a possible major obstacle for economic dynamics it is obvious for economic policy to look into the links of finance and the real sector of an economy and to try to find policy instruments to purposefully influence the economy.

Comparative studies of the situation in different countries produced at least two variant systems in use in the USA and continental Europe[3]. The former relies on a more market based financial system whereas in the latter a credit-based system is dominant. Both have advantages and disadvantages. However, it seems that in relation to fostering innovation a market based system is superior.

Deciding in favour of one system or changing one system necessitates the discussion as to whether there are systematic biases in the system leading to over- or underinvestment. Market failures may impede investment in some classes of firms (e.g. SMEs) or credit based systems may result in overinvestment in traditional industries because of too high risk averse attitudes of financial intermediaries or simply already long established customer relations. Thus the fundamental question of allocating investment in an economy is raised. Risk sharing and the possibility of appropriating gains from innovation turn out to be central questions to be solved when deciding on a proper financial framework.

---

[2]   The reader may consult one of several surveys of the developments of the Modigliani-Miller Theorem like Harris, Raviv (1991) to get a feeling of the theoretical developments alluded to.

[3]   See Allen (1995) for an example.

Smaller countries in particular are sensitive vis-à-vis foreign direct investment. The catch word "globalisation" has a threatening dimension for them in this context. They feel global competitive pressure but have only limited means to counter it. From their perspective they are fully open - that is unprotected - to the outside but have very limited chance to profit from the chances abroad, so for them the situation is very asymmetric. It is not astonishing that consequently in some European countries the mood is more like in a bunker than being ready for the take off into the information age.

Similarly the discussion of the behaviour of corporations under the heading "shareholder vs. stakeholder value" is leading to polarisation. Whether a company is maximising profits, improving the market value of the firm, or has a foremost obligation to care for the interests of its employees has an important implication for corporate finance and the competitive position of a firm.

The OECD set out to study the links between innovation and financial systems. The OECD study (1995) summarised nine propositions:

> "1) innovation is not a specialised economic activity but the mainspring of economic development;
> 2) to innovate is to invest;
> 3) the content of innovation-related investment and the uncertainties about its deployment create financing problems;
> 4) these problems cannot usefully be analysed in isolation from more general problems on the reconciliation of financial and industrial logics;
> 5) this reconciliation takes different forms in different countries;
> 6) the resulting national financing systems (including the role of government finance) have strong specificities corresponding to particular technological specialisations;
> 7) deregulation and globalisation of financial markets facilitate the finance of some types of investment but tend to destabilise national financing systems and do not always steer them automatically towards the most urgent structural adjustment tasks;
> 8) in the absence of adaptation, a dual systems + markets failure may create chronic insufficiency in innovation-related investment;

9) this insufficiency may affect the level of investment and its content (e.g. material versus immaterial), orientation (e.g. process versus product innovation), and distribution (e.g. SMEs versus large firms)"[4].

At least two areas to find new ways of finance for SME and especially start up companies are venture capital and market based financing via new stock exchanges or new segments of existing stock exchanges. Because of the huge success of venture capitalists in the USA a number of attempts have been made to use this method to increase the technological dynamics in Europe. It turned out, however, that it is more difficult than thought to duplicate this construction, although there has been ample capital available.

The venture capital sector is very differently developed in Europe.

Table 1: Countries ranked according to venture capital intensity as a propor tion of GNP (United Kingdom =100)

United Kingdom	100
Ireland	44
Netherlands	35
France	31
Sweden	27
Belgium	25
Italy	21
Norway	15
Germany	14
Portugal	13
Spain	13
Denmark	13
Switzerland	10
Finland	9
Greece	2
Austria	2

Source: Investors Chronicle, 22 October 1993[5].

---

[4]   OECD (1995), 12.
[5]   Quoted from OECD (1997), p. 42.

Another institution in the USA, which has inspired European efforts, is NASDAQ (National Association of Security Dealers Automated Quotation). From EASDAQ's (European Association of Securities Dealers Automated Quotation) homepage are the following quotes.

First from the Description of EASDAQ the first paragraphs of the introduction quoted from the webpage at url *http://www.easdaq.be/descript.html*:

> "EASDAQ has been created to bring together high-growth enterprise companies, their investors and financial intermediaries into one highly liquid, well-regulated, pan-European stock market.
> With admission to EASDAQ, companies will have direct access to, and increased profile with, a wider range of capital sources than can be found in any one national stock market. For institutional and private investors, the creation of EASDAQ means the ability to invest and trade directly in the shares of foreign companies without the problems and costs associated with cross-border share transactions on domestic markets.
> Based in Brussels, EASDAQ is a screen-based market which uses a multiple market-making system similar to that used by NASDAQ in the United States. Price quotation takes place using a state-of-the-art computerised trading platform created specifically for EASDAQ.
> EASDAQ has been set up and financed by a large group of financial intermediaries from across the European Union and the United States. Over 90 shareholders have funded the market's development. The market is independent of existing European stock markets.
> EASDAQ has high standards of regulation. It is authorised by the Belgian Banking and Finance Commission. Recent European Union directives mean authorisation in Belgium permits EASDAQ to operate its trading system in all other member states. Furthermore, the EASDAQ Rule Book has been closely modelled on NASDAQ's rules, allowing companies to comply with the information requirements of the Securities and Exchange Commission (SEC) in the United States and hence easily allowing companies to dual list on both NASDAQ and EASDAQ.
> EASDAQ's mission is to develop and operate a well-regulated, pan-European stock market which is liquid, efficient and fair, where fast-growing companies with international aspirations can raise capital from investors. In achieving its mission, EASDAQ will contribute to a stronger and more competitive European economy and so contribute to the creation of jobs and wealth for its people".

The use and present scope of EASDAQ is illustrated next again downloaded from the above homepage:

Key Market Statistics

COMPANY [1]	BUSINESS ACTIVITY	FIRST TRADING DATE	SPONSOR	ISSUE TYPE	CRN	MONEY RAISED AT ADMISSION (in ,000)	MARKET CAPITALI-SATION AT ADMISSION (in ,000)
ActivCard (Ordinary Shares) France	Computer Security	20/12/96	HQEM [2]	EASDAQ IPO	USD	11,200	109,729.736
Algol (Ordinary Shares) Italy	IT Distibution	20/11/97	Crédit Lyonnais	EASDAQ IPO	ITL[13]	13,800,000	30,000,000
Artwork Syst. (Ordinary Shares) Belgium	Computer Software	11/12/96	KB Securities	EASDAQ IPO	USD	51,252.338	178,269
Chemunex (Ordinary Shares) France	Microbio-logy Testing Sys.	25/3/97	Nomura Int'l	EASDAQ IPO	FRF[8]	151,000.2	424,893.474
City Bird Holding(Ordi-nary Shares) Belgium	Airline	05/11/97	Générale de Banque	EASDAQ IPO	USD	40,000	63,941.472
Debonair Hldgs (Ordinary Shares) UK	Airline	25/07/97	Crédit Lyonnais	EASDAQ IPO	GBP[10]	25,650	45,670.5
Dr. Solomon's (ADS) [3] England/Wales	Computer Software	27/11/96	HQEM [2]	Dual IPO Dual trading	USD	111,435	313,423.333
EDAP TMS (ADS) France	Medical Devices	01/08/97	Beeson Gregory	Dual IPO Dual trading	USD	36,000	78,196.5
Esat Telecom (ADS) Ireland	Telecom	07/11/97	Crédit Suisse First Boston	Dual IPO	USD	89,700	225,650.1
Espace Prod. Int. (Ordinary Shares) France	Construc-tion Materials	26/09/97	JP Pinatton	EASDAQ IPO	FRF	70,000.04	301,000.04
Esprit Telecom (ADS) [4] England/Wales	Telecom	28/02/97	Beeson Gregory	Dual IPO Dual trading	USD	57,000	205,801.284

.../...

Gruppo Formula (Ordinary Shares) Italy	Computer Software	03/11/97	Mediosim	EASDAQ IPO	ITL[12]	22,500,000	67,500,000
Innogenetics (Ordinary Shares) Belgium	Biotech.	28/11/96	KB Securities	EASDAQ IPO	USD	79,896.6	245,826.12
Integr. Surg. Syst. (Ordinary Shares) USA	Surgical Systems	21/11/97	CA IB Investment bank	EASDAQ PO	DEM[14]	18,000	65,889.732
Lernout & Hauspie (Ordi nary Shares) Belgium	Speech Products	23/06/97	Banque Paribas	Dual trading	USD	108,000 *	394,853.395
Melexis(Ordinary Shares) Belgium	Semi Conductors	10/10/97	Banque Paribas	EASDAQ IPO	USD	65,700	410,400
Mercer Int'l (Ordinary Shares) Switzerland [5]	Pulp & Paper	17/01/97	CA IB Investment bank	Dual trading	USD	none	162,767.418
NTL (Ordinary Shares) USA	Integrated Media	02/07/97	Mees Pierson	Dual trading	USD	none	802,439.175
Option Int'l (Ordinary Shares) Belgium	Modem Producers	26/11/97	Générale de Banque	EASDAQ IPO	USD	25,678.04	59,589.56
PixTech (Ordinary Shares) USA [6]	Flat Panel Display tech.	04/02/97	HQEM[2] Crédit Lyonnais	EASDAQ PO Dual trading	USD	17,982	54,617.157
Schoeller-Bleck. (Ordinary Shares) Austria	Oilfield Equipment	20/06/97	CA IB Investment bank	EASDAQ IPO	ATS[7]	420,000	1,407,000
Topcall Int'l (Ordinary Shares) Austria	Integrated IT	11/07/97	CA IB Investment bank	EASDAQ IPO	ATS[9]	493,050	855,000
Turbodyne Tech. (Ordinary Shares) Canada	Automotive	30/7/97	CA IB Investment bank	Dual trading	USD	none	113,922.849
TOTAL	(USD Equivalent)					880,726,321	3,900,573,274

1   The security name is the Master Issuer name
2   Hambrecht & Quist Euromarkets
3   American Depository Shares - 1 ADS represents three ordinary shares
4   American Depository Shares - 1 ADS represents seven ordinary shares
5   Principal Executive Office is located in Switzerland - Country of incorporation is USA
6   Principal Executive Office is located in France
7   Exchange rate ATS/USD: 12.1595
8   Exchange rate FRF/USD: 5.6968

9   Exchange rate ATS/USD: 12.4470
10   Exchange rate GBP/USD: 1.6615
11   Exchange rate FRF/USD: 5.909
12   Exchange rate ITL/USD: 1,700.1
13   Exchange rate ITL/USD: 1,694
14   Exchange rate DEM/USD: 1.734
*   The capital increase was done at USD 45.00 per share on 24/09/1997

It is still too early to come up with a final verdict about the success of EASDAQ. Much depends on the role and involvement of financial intermediaries acting as sponsors and market makers. If competition at a European or even global level prevents them from selecting market activities according to their business interests only, EASDAQ may prove to be an interesting new source of finance for companies enhancing European innovation.

Summing up it is surprising that despite deregulation and globalization of financial markets there are still important barriers for allocating financial means in a way to maximise aid for technological developments and improve economic conditions and competitiveness in Europe. There have to be principal reasons for the difficulties alluded to and it is best to study the situation by approaching the problem in a simplified framework.

3. Some observations on the role of asymmetric information in financial intermediation

Theoretical research has established the important role of information for economic decision making and economic activities. The seminal paper of Akerlof (1970) started research of asymmetries in the distribution of knowledge for the functioning of markets and derived rather dramatic consequences, which are by now well known. During the last decades a number of important insights have been gained concerning the implications of such asymmetries[6]. Although, at first, research concentrated on markets for goods and industrial economics, very soon interesting results for financial markets were presented. The following discussion is limited to the basic feature of the standard model used and one example of a possibility to overcome asymmetric information.

A. Actors

It is best to start with the agents being active in the model. There are units having financial means available which they would like to invest. These agents will be called investors. Others are looking for funds; they are short of financial means. Traditionally these are entrepreneurs. The process of bringing together funds to be invested and investment opportunities, that is investors and entrepreneurs, is called financial intermediation. As already mentioned capital markets may perform the intermediating function, sometimes in competition with special agents called financial intermediaries. For simplicity it is assumed that only specialised units, the financial intermediaries, can perform intermediation. Still further simplifying one can assume that there exists only one representative of each group.

This set-up abstracts from all competitive rivalry among the three groups and allows the study of the simplest cases. Two basic channels will be discussed. One is a direct investment channel where the investor supplies capital directly to the entrepreneur. The other one is the case of intermediation[7].

B. Basic assumptions

The standard decision problem in this respect is one under uncertainty. The project, which needs to be financed, produces a return, which can be reaped in the future only and is therefore uncertain. What do the actors know about the quality of the project? It is natural to assume that the entrepreneur who wants

---

6   For the following discussion see Freixas, Rochet (1997).
7   A recent survey is in Bhattacharya, Thakor (1993).

to carry out the project is better informed about the quality of the project than the investor resulting in an informational asymmetry.

C.   Some results

As it is one of the important results concerning asymmetric information *adverse selection* will be outlined here. Assume that investors face a large number of entrepreneurs each having a project with expected return R_i and variance $\acute{o}^2$ being the same for all projects. R_i is private information of entrepreneur i. Assuming that in equilibrium the price of equity P will be the same for all firms it is easy to see that only firms with low quality (return) projects are selling these to the market, that is firm i selling is if

$$R_i < P, \quad (3)$$

whereas all others would break even at best[8].

This situation may lead to a break-down of the market mechanism because investors would almost certainly lose money on their investment and would not be ready to pay the price P that therefore cannot be an equilibrium.

In order to induce investors to finance projects entrepreneurs have to do something to enhance investors' trust. One way to do this is to finance the project only partly by outside money. The entrepreneur retains a certain amount of his project and sells part $\acute{a}$ to investors. Investors take $\acute{a}$ as a signal for the entrepreneur's credibility. They have to be aware, however, that entrepreneurs may try to portray their projects to have a higher quality than they know.

Thus the amount of $\acute{a}$ can be inferred from the market equilibrium, because $\acute{a}$ has to be large enough to induce investors to buy the part of the project offered by the entrepreneurs. On the other hand it must be true that the entrepreneur

---

[8]   This is Akerlof's result.

has an inducement to sell his project. Therefore $\acute{a}$ depends on the distribution of R_i and the preferences of investors and entrepreneurs[9].

For SMEs signalling by using self-financing seems to be an important strategy to raise capital from investors and to overcome informational asymmetries.

The existence of intermediaries changes the situation and adds an *incentive problem*. If the intermediary offers to *monitor* the efforts of entrepreneurs it may save costs for the investors. In addition a financial intermediary may provide higher quality monitoring because of scale effects and specialisation. Despite these advantages the investor may have to monitor the monitor and find means to ensure that the financial intermediary is performing its task well (a so-called *principal-agent problem*).

It is obvious that a developed financial sector typically offers both channels to finance projects. An analysis of an elaborated financial system is much more complex and beyond the scope of this chapter. However, it should be noted, that SMEs may be at a disadvantage in both cases whether they use capital markets or financial intermediaries.

4.   Conclusions

The importance of SMEs for economic dynamics is established beyond doubt. Therefore it is necessary to secure an optimal environment for this class of firms in order to influence growth and technological progress in an economy. Although nobody denies these arguments, the working of economic institutions very often gives rise to complaints from SMEs.

As section 3 demonstrates, the complexity of economic problems leads to implicit barriers, which generate problems that are more onerous for SMEs than large corporations. Different branches of economic theory try to contribute to the understanding of these difficulties and to come up with solutions. Among these

---

[9]   Leland, Pyle (1977) introduced signalling into the analysis of intermediation.

branches the theory of capital structure and industrial economics play an important role especially with models of situation of asymmetric information. In addition, recent research on the process of financial intermediation has generated a better understanding of the working of credit finance based systems as well as the important role of regulation of the financial sector[10].

Economic policy is searching for solutions to the urgent need to foster competitiveness of European economies[11]. Because of the difficulty of the task it will take some time till positive impacts of the policy attempts will be felt.

---

[10]   See Schäfer (1997) for interesting results concerning deposit insurance.
[11]   An example for the pragmatic approach followed is OECD (1997).

Résumé

L'asymétrie d'information, source de problèmes pour le financement des petites et moyennes entreprises (PME)

Les études portant sur la croissance économique ont clairement mis en évidence le rôle majeur du progrès technique. Partant du niveau macro-économique les analyses en la matière se sont déplacées vers le niveau micro-économique de l'entreprise, mettant notamment l'accent sur la distinction entre invention et innovation. Quel que soit le rôle de l'entrepreneur, le progrès technique est en général reconnu comme un instrument de politique économique.

Dans tous les pays industriels on observe que les PME participent activement à la dynamique du développement économique. Ce constat fonde dès lors l'intérêt que l'on porte aux PME et à la promotion de l'esprit d'entreprise. Dans beaucoup de pays le financement de la création d'entreprises, ou du développement de PME, demeure cependant problématique. C'est donc vers les modalités de financement de ces entreprises que s'est déplacée l'attention des chercheurs et des acteurs de l'économie.

Les pratiques américaines sont souvent analysées sous un angle comparatif et ont tendance à servir de référence ; c'est ainsi que le NASDAQ a inspiré l'EASDAQ.

Mais l'efficience des marchés financiers est limitée par une série de facteurs de base parmi lesquels il faut mentionner l'asymétrie de l'information. L'allocation optimale de ressources s'en trouve biaisée au détriment des PME. La crédibilité de celles-ci est aussi mise en doute par les intermédiaires financiers. Face à la complexité de ces problèmes la politique économique est conduite d'une manière pragmatique.

Hanns A. ABELE

Zusammenfassung

Asymmetrische Informationen als Problem der Finanzierung von Klein- und Mittelbetrieben

Die Studien zum Wirtschaftswachstum haben die Bedeutung des technischen Fortschritts klargemacht. Ursprünglich war dies eher eine makroökonomische Betrachtung. Genauere Analysen des technischen Fortschritts haben schließlich Erfindung und Innovation unterschieden. Daher hat sich die Analyse auf Unternehmensebene verlagert. Zugleich wurde die Rolle des technischen Fortschritts auch als wirtschaftspolitisches Instrument erkannt.

Da in allen Industrieländern Klein- und Mittelbetriebe wesentlich die wirtschaftliche Dynamik mitbestimmen, heißt die wirtschaftspolitische Richtschnur, Förderung von Klein- und Mittelbetrieben. In vielen Wirtschaften ist für solche Unternehmen jedoch die Finanzierung neuer Vorhaben oder überhaupt die Finanzierung von Neugründungen ein Problem, weshalb das Studium der Finanzierungbedingungen in das Zentrum des Interesses gerückt ist.

Um Verbesserungen zu erreichen, werden vergleichende Untersuchungen gemacht. Dabei sind amerikanische Methoden oftmals beispielgebend. Deshalb wurden Maßnahmen ergriffen, um die amerikanischen Erfahrungen zumindest teilweise nutzbringend anwenden zu können (z.B. Gründung der EASDAQ).

Allerdings gibt es grundsätzliche Schwierigkeiten, die das Funktionieren des Finanzsektors behindern. Dazu gehört insbesondere die Auswirkung asymmetrischer Informationen. Sucht ein Unternehmer für ein Projekt eine Finanzierung, weiß er zumeist besser als potentielle Geldgeber, wie die Erfolgsaussichten seines Vorhabens stehen. In solchen Fällen, so hat die Theorie gezeigt, kann der Marktmechanismus zusammenbrechen. Ein Ausweg wäre, wenn der Unternehmer seine Glaubwürdigkeit durch eine entsprechende Eigenfinanzierung unterstreicht. Aber auch bei Finanzierung durch Finanzintermediäre kann es Probleme geben.

Als Ausweg für die Wirtschaftspolitik angesichts der Komplexität der Probleme aber auch der Handlungsnotwendigkeit bietet sich ein pragmatisches Vorgehen an.

References

ADAMS, W./DIRLAM, J.B. (1966): Big Steel, Invention, and Innovation. *The Quarterly Journal of Economics*, 80(2). 167-189.

ADAMS, W./DIRLAM, J.B. (1967): Big Steel, Invention and Innovation: Reply. *The Quarterly Journal of Economics*, 81(3). 475-482.

AKERLOF, G. (1970): The Market for Lemons: Quality Uncertainty and the Market Mechanism. *The Quarterly Journal of Economics*, 84(3). 488-500.

ALLEN, F. (1995): Stock Markets and Resource Allocation. in: MAYER, C./ VIVES, X. (eds.): *Capital Markets and Financial Intermediation*. Cambridge. 81-116.

BHATTACHARYA, S./THAKOR, A.V. (1993): Contemporary Banking Theory. *Journal of Financial Intermediation* 3(1). 2-50.

FREIXAS, X./ROCHET, J.-C. (1997): *Microeconomics of Banking*. Cambridge, Mass. London.

HARRIS, M./RAVIV, A. (1991): The Theory of Capital Structure. *Journal of Finance* 46(1). 297-355.

LELAND, H.E./PYLE, D.H. (1977): Informational Asymmetries, Financial Structure, and Financial Intermediation. *Journal of Finance*, 32(2). 371-387.

MAS-COLLEL, A./WHINSTON, M.D./GREEN, J.R. (1995): *Microeconomic Theory*. Oxford e.a.

McADAMS, H.K. (1967): Big Steel, Invention, and Innovation Reconsidered. *The Quarterly Journal of Economics*, 81(3). 457-474.

OECD (1995): *National Systems for Financing Innovation*. Paris.

OECD (1997): *Best Practice Policies for Small and Medium-Sized Enterprises*. Paris.

SCHÄFER, G. (1997): *Essays on Banking Regulation*. Ph.D. Thesis. University of Economics and Business Administration Vienna.

Sabine Urban (ed.)

Europe in the Global Competition

Problems – Markets – Strategies

1997, 339 pages, DM 89,– (approx. US $ 48.19)
ISBN 3-409-13434-4

The global environment is characterized by an increasing dynamism. In this highly competitive situation Europe has to implement appropriate strategies and techniques.

In "Europe in the Global Competition" renowned academics analyze strengths and weaknessses of the European Union against the background of world economy and discuss its role in the global competition from different perspectives. Topics are:

– globalization,
– unemployment,
– market economy and the principle of commonweal,
– competitiveness and
– insurance.

Students and professors of business administration, research centers and European organizations gain a critical and comparative vision of the European reality. This publication of the Centre d'Etude des Sciences Appliquées à la Gestion at Strasbourg University-IECS also gives constructive suggestions.

Betriebswirtschaftlicher Verlag Dr. Th. Gabler GmbH, Abraham-Lincoln-Str. 46, 65189 Wiesbaden